Living with the
Black Dog

Living with the

Black Dog

How to cope when your partner is depressed

Caroline Carr

Editor: Roni Jay

new tricks for old dogs

Published by White Ladder Press Ltd
Great Ambrook, Near Ipplepen, Devon TQ12 5UL

01803 813343

www.whiteladderpress.com

First published in Great Britain in 2007

10 9 8 7 6 5 4 3 2 1

13-digit ISBN 978 1 90541010 1

British Library Cataloguing in Publication Data
A CIP record for this book can be obtained from the British Library.

Designed and typeset by Julie Martin Ltd
Cover design by Julie Martin Ltd
Cover photograph Jonathon Bosley
Printed and bound by TJ International Ltd, Padstow, Cornwall
Cover printed by St Austell Printing Company
Printed on totally chlorine-free paper
FSC (The Forest Stewardship Council) is an international
network to promote responsible management of the world's forests.

FSC

Mixed Sources
Product group from well-managed
forests and other controlled sources

Cert no. SGS-COC-2482
www.fsc.org
© 1996 Forest Stewardship Council

White Ladder Press Ltd
Great Ambrook, Near Ipplepen, Devon TQ12 5UL
01803 813343

Contents

Acknowledgements

With love and respect to ND, EG, and GL.

Thank you to Wendy and John for their continuous, unconditional love and support.

A note from the author

You may find it useful to visit my website **www.carolinecarr.com** which contains further information and support, and where you can share your own experiences of living with someone who is depressed. Alternatively, you can email me at **enquiries@caro-linecarr.com**. I look forward to hearing from you.

"Crippling depression and chronic anxiety are the biggest causes of misery in Britain today. They are the great submerged problem, which shame keeps out of sight. But if you mention them, you soon discover how many families are affected. According to the respected Psychiatric Morbidity Survey, one in six of us would be diagnosed as having depression or chronic anxiety disorder, which means that one family in three is affected."

Professor Lord Richard Layard *The Depression Report – A New Deal for Depression and Anxiety Disorders*
http://cep.lse.ac.uk/textonly/research/mentalhealth/DEPRESSION_R EPORT_LAYARD.pdf published June 2006 by The Centre for Economic Performance, London School of Economics and Political Science (**http://cep.lse.ac**)

Introduction

When I was about four, my cousin said he'd beat me up unless I stole a rose from every garden in our lane. As he was older and taller than I was, I duly obeyed. When my mother found out, she was furious with us both. She promptly marched me up the lane and made me say sorry as I returned each flower to its owner.

Most of our neighbours looked stern but forgave me on the spot. Then we got to Aggie Armstrong's. Aggie was my favourite neighbour. She seemed to bake continually, and her house had a delectable aroma of bread, pies and cakes. Always friendly and welcoming, she often let me sample something she'd made. At worst, I always got a sweet. I saw her as a pillar of stability. For a start, there was plenty of her. She had a large bosom and arms, and a smooth round face which was usually smiling.

However, this time it was completely different. She didn't seem to notice me at all. Her eyes were red and swollen, and she seemed preoccupied.

"It's Ted," she said to my mother, shaking her head. "That black dog's at him again, the cruel bastard." at which point she burst into tears.

"What black dog?" I wondered, and what had it done to Ted?

The whole of her body shook as she pulled a large handkerchief out of her apron pocket and blew her nose. I was shocked to see this strong, solid woman in such a state. To see that kindly face

1

contorted with misery, water streaming from her eyes and nose, was disconcerting to say the least. Even then I knew that something was really wrong. I felt her pain. I saw her grief and desperation, and I heard her sobs.

Ted, it seemed, had taken to his bed and had been there for three days. He refused to have the curtains open, and he had hardly said a word to Aggie in all that time. He had no interest in the meals she'd made him, and he wouldn't see a doctor as he didn't want any of "those bloody pills". She was distraught.

Later my mother explained that sometimes Ted was ill with a thing called 'depression'. She told me that an important person called Winston Churchill had also had depression, and that he called it his black dog.

Years later I understood what Aggie had meant. To her, "that black dog" was also a "cruel bastard".

Chapter 1

Suddenly, Jim barged into the kitchen and burst into tears.

"I hope we're doing the right thing," he wailed.

"Good grief," I thought, "what's the matter with him?" I stopped washing up and gave him a hug. "Hey – it's OK. Of course we're doing the right thing. It'll all be fine."

He pulled himself away and slumped in a chair.

"I just want everything to work out for the best. That's all." he sobbed. As I sat down next to him I felt bewildered and helpless. Jim and I had been together for twenty years, and in that time I had rarely seen him cry. As I tried to comfort him, I began to realise that something was really wrong. Actually, I had been puzzled by his behaviour for some time. Now it occurred to me – perhaps it had all been building up to this. His tears gradually subsided, but he remained in a low mood all day. He didn't sleep much that night. The next day he just lay on the settee, dozing or staring into space.

We had just moved house and our daughters had started new schools. Everything had seemed fine, but that day it all started to change. Over the next few weeks, I became more and more worried by his behaviour. He started to seek me out – wherever I was in the house – to tell me how miserable he felt, and how we'd made a huge mistake in moving house.

"We shouldn't have done it." He'd wail. "We've made a terrible mistake."

"No we haven't." I'd think to myself. "He's being ridiculous."

On the surface I remained calm, but inside, I was really worried. Jim's mental state was affecting us all. Often the girls would come home from school to find him standing in the hallway tearful and apologetic.

"I'm sorry, I'm so sorry." he'd weep. This bothered them. What on earth was he sorry about? Here he was, their dad, very upset. Every day. They wondered why. They had enough to cope with – new schools, making new friends, experiencing new emotions themselves – without this.

During those weeks I spent hours listening to Jim's tales of woe. These sessions could continue well into the night. His negativity and moaning seemed endless. His view of the world seemed to be squashed together into a soggy grey blob of misery. At some stage I delicately suggested that he might like to get some professional help, and eventually, with a look of forlorn resignation, he agreed to see a doctor. He was officially diagnosed as being clinically depressed and started to see a psychiatrist and a counsellor regularly.

"Thank God." I thought. "Perhaps he'll start getting better now."

He was prescribed tablets, which he flushed down the toilet.

"I'm not having those – I don't need them." he said.

"Well how's things going with your counsellor?" I asked.

"OK."

One day he came back from talking to her, and smiled at me sadly.

"She thinks I am the most depressed person she has ever seen."

The girls and I supported each other by talking about him. Not to him – but about him –when he wasn't there. We wanted to help him, but nothing we said or did seemed to make any difference at all. He was depressed, and was wearing it like a badge. We were confused by his behaviour, and his constant moping. Secretly we referred to him as Eeyore, after the morose donkey in *Winnie the Pooh*.

Then gradually, the rot really set in. The tears stopped, and were replaced by rage – and it was all directed at me. Instead of sorrow and sadness there was an atmosphere of angst, of a person tormented; almost deranged. I could feel his hatred and anger. Eeyore metamorphosed into something else.

Jim followed me around like someone possessed. I became the focus of his tirades of expletives and accusations. These exhibitions could occur at any time of day or night, and anything seemed to trigger them. Like the time I came home from a particularly busy day at work.

"Hi." I said brightly. Within seconds he was there. He stood in front of me glaring.

"I've had a bloody awful day. It never used to be as bad as this. I wish I'd never listened to you. You manipulated me. You made us move…" He went on.

"It's your fault. You always get your own way. I shouldn't have listened to you…" My heart sank and my stomach felt as if it had jumped up to meet it, doing a double flip on the way.

"Jim, I'm so sorry you feel like this." I said. "Leave me alone – please." I thought as I walked away. He followed me into the kitchen.

"You make me sick. You think you're not going to listen to me – well you are, 'cos it's about time you did. You had it all worked out. You made us move…" He went on and on.

Often the girls would see and hear these outbursts. It was frightening for them. They'd say afterwards: "Mum, why does he have a go at you? It's not true what he says – you're not that bad."

I had to keep telling them that no, I wasn't that bad. This really wasn't about me. It was Dad's illness that was making him behave like this.

But secretly, I began to wonder. What had I done? *Was* it my fault that we'd moved? After all, we'd planned the whole thing together. But now, in his mind, everything seemed to be my fault. He talked at me – repeating himself over and over again – accusing me of manipulating him and being selfish, and not caring. I felt like I was being brainwashed. There was never any physical violence. If there had been, I would have left like a shot, taking the girls with me. But I knew that he was ill, and that he was getting help. As it happened, *I* needed help too.

The key feature of this book is you. How *you* can cope when you live with someone who is depressed, and what *you* can do to stop yourself being dragged down into their pit of despair.

The first piece of advice that you are likely to hear from anyone who has your best interests at heart is: "Look after yourself, won't you?" That *is* great advice – but how on earth are you supposed to do that when your world is caving in around you and you are in emotional turmoil?

The ideas and tips in this book have all been tried and tested by people who have lived with someone who is depressed. Some may work better for you than others – and that's fine. All the case studies given are real, though of course the names have been changed.

Some of the ideas will suggest that you use your imagination, or that you visualise something. If you are one of the many people who doesn't actually *see* something in your mind's eye, that is perfectly fine. Perhaps you just *know* instead. So just do it in whatever way works for you.

Keep an open mind. You need to keep yourself sane, safe and healthy. Allow yourself to be creative. Experiment, and be a little wicked if you need to be. Above all, realise that you are not alone.

If your partner is depressed, their behaviour is likely to have an effect on you (and your family). Therefore:

- You need to understand something of how depression may be affecting your partner.

- You need some skills and strategies that will help you to cope.

- You can then make choices about how you can best handle the situation you are in.

Chapter 2

Jim was the wittiest, most tolerant and gentle man I'd ever met. We had lots in common, he was great company and I loved him. We married, we had babies. Life was really good. Sometimes he was a little melancholic, but that didn't bother me – my positive take on life could usually lift his spirits, and all would be well again. OK, life had dealt him some blows, but it had also given him some wonderful things, so when he grumbled, I'd think to myself, "Yes, I know – life can be a bitch. Now get over it."

Years later, his melancholic moments increased to longer periods of gloom. Later still, when Jim was diagnosed as being clinically depressed, it dawned on me that it must have been building up for some time. I realised that there'd been subtle warning signs for two or three years previously. There had been changes in his profession and he began to get less work. Projects that he started did not succeed as he wished. His confidence in his own abilities dwindled, and his self-esteem was generally low. I noticed that he grumbled more often and more regularly. He'd become far less tolerant of all sorts of things. At the time I thought he was just being awkward, so I didn't pay too much attention.

Sometimes, alarm bells sounded in my head. I think I merely acknowledged and then disregarded them, putting my thoughts about them on hold. I suppose it was like filing memories away in a computer, or stuffing them in a drawer in case I needed to refer to them again later.

For example, we were invited to dinner at a friend's house one evening. I thought we'd both been looking forward to it. It would be the first time we had all had dinner together – there would only be the four of us, and it would be very casual. Another friend was babysitting so everything was sorted out – or so I thought. But an hour before we were due to leave, Jim said:

"Look, I've spent the whole day feeling fed up. I just don't feel up to going. But you go. I haven't got much in common with them anyway, and you know them better than I do." So at the last minute, the babysitter was cancelled, and I went off to dinner without him. I felt slightly embarrassed as I made up some paltry excuse for his absence. But I missed him being there.

As the months went on, I was aware that things were changing. Jim's low moods seemed to last for longer, and he was quick to apportion blame in various directions. In his view, it was always someone's fault that he felt as he did. I got a sense that he felt like a victim, and he adopted a really fatalistic turn of phrase. He'd say things like:

"I just stagger from one crisis to another."
"Knowing my luck…"
"I'm jinxed."

I noticed he'd become obsessive about some things, and would not let the matter drop.

For example, he became increasingly disturbed by the neighbours. They were "too noisy". He couldn't "stand that woman's voice." But they *weren't* noisy. Yes, they had a baby, and sometimes we could hear him cry. We heard his mother comforting him and playing with him. But it wasn't noisy. To Jim though, it was unbearable. So much so, that he soundproofed the wall between our house and theirs.

Then there were the mornings. I became exasperated by his behaviour then. Usually I woke up in a cheerful mood and opened the bedroom curtains. Over the years, I'd got used to being greeted with a "good morning" and a kiss. But now, Jim woke up and groaned each morning. He put his hand over his eyes like Dracula at dawn. He'd listen in trepidation for the post. As it came through the letter box he'd moan:

"Oh no – another day of bad news." Or: "Another wad of bills". I was genuinely puzzled. I really thought he was being ridiculous – and selfish. I couldn't understand what he was so bothered about. I was fed up with his miserable attitude each morning.

When you are around a partner who becomes increasingly negative or irrational in their thinking or behaviour, you will be affected in some way. A range of things can happen:

:‍: You are likely to become confused and worried

:‍: You may wonder if it's your fault

:‍: You may find that you seem to be unable to help them

:‍: They sap your energy like a vampire and you start to feel low yourself

:‍: You feel angry and resentful, and you blame them

:‍: You also may feel a huge burden of guilt, and a certain amount of shame

You may not be able to help your partner to challenge their thinking, or change their behaviour, but you *can* stop yourself being dragged down and sliding into similar patterns of negativity.

I just carried on with my life as usual. I was occupied most of the time with the children and part-time work, and I had a pleasant social life with some good friends. I also went for plenty of long walks by myself, and felt better for the fresh air.

The thing is – I used the walking time to think. I churned things over in my mind, again and again. That was exhausting.

What you can do to help yourself:

Talk to someone. I didn't do this, and I think it might have helped me to see what was happening, and to stop churning things over in my mind so much. I would have felt disloyal and embarrassed discussing Jim with friends – which is probably why I didn't. However, there are help lines that you can phone and yet remain anonymous. You could also speak to your GP.

If alarm bells are ringing in your head – *listen to them.* If you ignore them they may not go away. Share your concerns with someone else. There is no question about making a fuss or looking stupid. One conversation with the right person may just stop the ringing of alarm bells from developing into an almighty clanging.

Though I didn't realise it at the time, Jim was becoming quite seriously depressed. People have since been very empathic and said things like:

"Oh that must have been awful for you…"

Well, yes it was. However, others go through far worse – watching someone they love harm themselves repeatedly, for example. So I need to draw a distinction between the depression that Jim experienced, and that of others.

Neurotic disorder includes depression or an anxiety disorder. The depression that Jim experienced fell into this category. Most of us experience low mood states sometimes, but a great many people do actually become depressed.

Psychosis is where a person's perception of the world is distorted by, for example, delusions and hallucinations. Disorders such as manic depression (bipolar disorder) and schizophrenia fall into this category.

As a person becomes depressed they tend to become much more rigid in their thinking. They cease to be flexible and open to ideas and possibilities. They become fixed into a pattern of thoughts and feelings which are unhelpful, and often they can see no way out. When someone is really depressed they seem to expect the worst all the time. It's as if life has been specially designed to disappoint them, and so this is exactly what happens.

They become locked into a cycle of negative thoughts, feelings and behaviour.

In order to explain how this works, I will offer these as definitions:

Thoughts are what you tell yourself in your head (your self-talk). They are based on your beliefs about the world, and how you interpret a situation or feeling.

Feelings are – well, what you feel. Your emotions, such as sad, happy, anxious, excited. They come about as a response to a situation or a thought. They create a sensation and a reaction in your mind and body.

Behaviour is what you actually do, the action you do or do not take.

Which comes first – thought or feeling?

One school of thought says that the way you *think* affects the way you *feel*, which affects the way you *behave*. Another school of thought says that the way you *feel* affects the way you *think*, which affects the way you behave. Most seem to agree that the way you behave will be as a result of what you think and feel.

Basically, the main thing to realise is that thoughts, feelings and behaviour are inextricably linked. If you change one, it will have an effect on the others.

If your thoughts are positive – that's great. You attract good things, because you're open to them. Suppose your thought is "I'm having a great day." You feel happy, so you smile appropriately and chat pleasantly to people you meet. The chances are that you'll get a good response from them, and this in turn could lead to socializing, sharing of ideas, invitations, mutual friendliness and respect. And what does that do for you? How are you likely to think, feel and behave? I'll bet it's positive.

Like this:

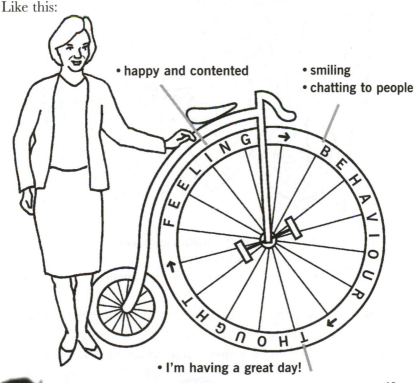

• happy and contented

• smiling
• chatting to people

FEELING

BEHAVIOUR

THOUGHT

• I'm having a great day!

On the other hand, if your thoughts are regularly gloomy, you can become locked in a cycle of negativity that can be tricky to break out of. You block yourself in areas of your life. For example, supposing you think certain people don't like you. You feel fed up about it and annoyed, so you might ignore them. What impression is that likely to give them? They probably decide they actually don't like you very much because of the way you behave towards them...

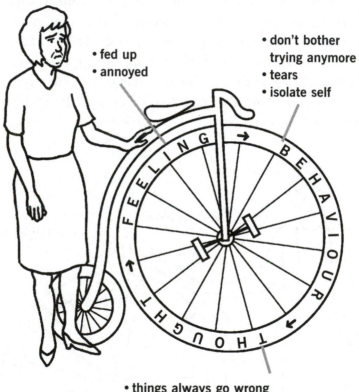

• fed up
• annoyed

• don't bother
  trying anymore
• tears
• isolate self

FEELING →

BEHAVIOUR

THOUGHT

• things always go wrong
• it's hopeless
• I can't do anything about it

...and so it goes on, round and round until something changes. And if you want it to change – you have to change. Otherwise you remain stuck in this pattern, and more importantly it could get worse. A person who is seriously depressed is likely to see no way out and puts a negative spin on everything. Their thinking shrinks inwards so that they focus entirely on the negative, and as this happens they can sink down into utter despondency.

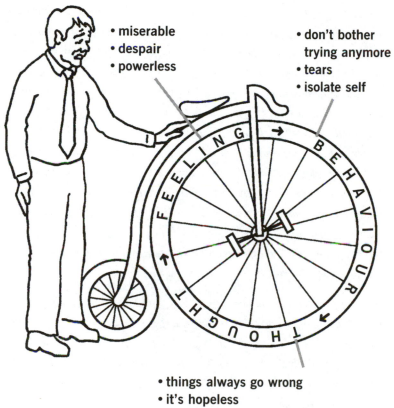

- miserable
- despair
- powerless

- don't bother trying anymore
- tears
- isolate self

- things always go wrong
- it's hopeless
- I can't do anything about it

When someone is firmly hooked into a pattern of negative thoughts and feelings it can be really tricky for them to change. With the best will in the world they will inevitably come up with a "yes, but" to anything positive. So they hang on to their limitations like a safety net. This is when a change in behaviour can make all the difference. It can be a catalyst for new positive thoughts and feelings to replace the old negative ones.

Brenda

Brenda was forty-five. Her partner John told me:

"Brenda and I nearly split up eight years ago. She wasn't really depressed – but I'd got so sick of her self-pity. She'd always wanted to teach little children, but she had no confidence in herself. She said that she'd hated school, and for her, it had been full of bad experiences. She described her schooling as "Like being in a fog". Often she didn't understand instructions, and always took longer than everyone else. There were all sorts of other things – she couldn't read the board easily, and if she was made to read out loud she stumbled and stuttered, and other kids laughed at her. One teacher even told her she was thick, so of course, she told herself that she wouldn't ever amount to much. I know she felt frustrated and angry. Well, anyway, she was always brilliant at designing things and art, but she always put herself down. It really got to me. I mean, we had two lovely kids, and we'd done all right, so why did she keep moaning? She bothered less with her appearance as time went on. I got so sick of it, I nearly left.

A friend persuaded her to join an art class, and this was a turning point. One of the tutors suggested that she get tested for dyslexia. Well – that's what it was. All those years, and we hadn't realised. Once she realised that she wasn't thick, she began to think differently about herself, and to cut a long story short, she's just qualified as a teacher. I'm so proud of her now – she's like a different person."

The word depression comes from the Latin *deprimere* which means pressed down. So: de-pressed.

Mental disorder and depression have been around for thousands of years, as have theories about why depression occurs and how to deal with it. At various times in history it is thought to have had something to do with the elements of earth, fire, water and air, the cycle of the moon, personality, witchcraft, religious beliefs, sin, the devil, the supernatural, nature spirits or animal spirits, and the struggle a person has with their conscience. Treatments have included things like exorcism, baths, bloodletting and whipping.

We now have masses of research and scientific evidence about depression. Depending on the severity and the symptoms, modern treatment in general Western medicine tends to be:

- Medication in the form of antidepressant drugs

- Psychotherapy, such as:

  - *Psychoanalysis* to explore the reasons why someone may have become depressed
  - *Counselling* to help people cope with problems they are experiencing.
  - *CBT (cognitive behavioural therapy)* which looks at the relationship between thoughts and feelings. It helps the person to see things in a different way, and to practice coping skills in situations that they find awkward

- ECT (electroconvulsive therapy) in specific cases where appropriate; this is where an electric shock is given to the brain

It is essential to realise how important it is to see the GP in the first instance. A doctor will be able to eliminate any other reasons that may be causing the symptoms of depression, such as another illness or infection, or the side-effects of some medication.

Chapter 3

Eventually, we decided to move. To start with, Jim was appre-
hensive. He had put a great deal of physical work into our house
in the country, and had made it into a really wonderful home for
us. But we both realised that we needed to be nearer a town.
There were lots of reasons, and the time seemed to be right.

So we sold the house, and bought another on the outskirts of a
town some miles away. We all seemed excited. I had visions of
discovering new places, doing new things, enjoying adventures
together. Surely this would give us all a boost. A new life, in fact.

*The life we got was not what I expected. Due to Jim's thorough planning
and preparation, the move went smoothly. However his reaction to the change
was far from smooth.*

Once someone who experienced depression described to me
how she felt, like this:

"You know how you go around in your own little bubble most of
the time – you feel OK and no one can sort of get 'at' you? Well
I feel as if my bubble's gone, and I'm wide open."

I thought that was a wonderful analogy, because really that's how
it is.

Imagine it like this:

**At best, you function within your own protective invisible bubble.
Your bubble surrounds you, and it is flexible and comfortable**

☺ It develops from qualities within you, such as self-esteem, confidence, warmth and general well-being

☺ It protects you, in that you are able to get on with your life without being too fazed by its ups and downs

☺ You have the capacity to enjoy and benefit from other people's company

☺ You can achieve

☺ You can appreciate the richness of life

This bubble is a wonderful thing to have – it's your personal protection insurance, it's flexible and it gives good value, as it keeps you mentally safe.

Your bubble can change into one that is hard and impenetrable

☹ This is because of the thoughts and feelings that you have, so you may surround yourself with a bubble for protection in a different way

☹ You may not want anyone to get any where near you, because you feel that you've been hurt or damaged

☹ People may want nothing to do with you because of the way you are, so they stay away; your bubble is as rigid as steel, and it does a fine job of keeping you isolated

Of course, you may be amongst people, but your bubble stops them from getting anywhere near the real you. Is that what you really want?

Sometimes, you may feel that you don't have a bubble surrounding you at all

☹ It may be that it just seems to have disappeared

☹ You might have been chipping away at it without even realising

☺ Perhaps you've absorbed the problems and issues of other people so much that your own recourses are worn down

☺ It may be that the verbal attack and constant negativity of others has exhausted you

☺ You may feel as if a lot of your inner recourses have left you, and you feel vulnerable and insecure

This is when you will feel wide open and unprotected, and notice the effects of events and situations in a more extreme way.

Someone who is depressed is likely to fit into either of the latter two categories. You, as the person who lives with them, need to make sure that you keep a comfortable bubble of protection around yourself at all times, otherwise their negativity can start to chip away at it until there seems to be nothing left. This can be easier said than done, and I think you have to work at it. You need that bubble to keep yourself sane, safe and healthy. All the suggestions in this book will help to keep your personal protection bubble intact.

One of the best ways to weaken your bubble is to receive a shock. Then – whoops! It gets you – a surge of emotion that hits you in the solar plexus, somewhere between your naval and your heart, and throws you off balance for a while. The behaviour of a depressed person can be a real shock to you. Their behaviour can leave you feeling 'all at sea' for a while, and unable to make the best decisions.

I was very familiar with this sensation when Jim was ill and angry. The mere thought of our situation could play havoc with my emotions. As soon as I thought about it, I felt as if I'd been winded. My face burned, and my voice changed completely, so that when I spoke, instead of my normal voice, I was aware of a strained, wobbly sound coming from somewhere deep in my throat. I didn't know whether I was coming or going for a while. I felt as if I'd been thrown off balance – physically and mental-ly. Each time I experienced these sensations, my safe protective bubble grew weaker. Thankfully I was aware of this, and found ways to cope, so that I did not lose my bubble altogether.

Every suggestion given in this book is a way to help you to keep your protective bubble around you. This may not seem particu-larly obvious, but that is exactly what you will be doing. You will be feeding it, building it around you, and encouraging it to stay.

Once, several years later, I told Jim what the woman with depres-sion had said. Looking utterly forlorn he said, "At least she had a bubble. I never had one."

Chapter 4

The girls and I moved out first. Jim wanted time on his own to leave things in order for the next vendors. I realised that this would probably be a particularly emotional time for him. He had put so much hard graft into the house – it was as if it was his baby. I knew that he would need time on his own to close this episode of his life, and to say goodbye to the place that held so many memories for us. *I didn't realise that it would be so hard for him to leave. It seemed as if he left a part of his heart and soul there that day.*

When Jim joined us the following afternoon, he seemed fine. We'd moved into temporary accommodation, and the girls and I had already unpacked the things we'd be likely to need for a month or two.

I was so excited at the prospect of our new life. I felt like a child who'd been given the best present ever. I saw the whole thing as an adventure, with new places to visit and new opportunities. The girls seemed just as happy. They wanted to explore – especially in all the high street shops, which were now nearby. I thought Jim was happy too. He seemed to be – but actually, either I misread the signals, or he was masking his true anxieties extremely well.

As soon as the computer was set up, he threw himself into his work. He seemed preoccupied and anxious. One day, I showed him an advert for a project that I thought might interest him in the local paper. I immediately wished I hadn't bothered.

"Surely you don't think I'm going to do that do you? What would I want to do that for?"

"How can he be so bloody arrogant?" I thought. I hated this attitude. I'd only meant to help. Why did he react as if I was trying to belittle him?

What I hadn't realised was that Jim was desperately grasping at straws. He was making a huge effort to maintain his own identity, at a time when he actually felt that he was swimming against the tide, and that he was losing control to the black dog: depression.

When someone is depressed, their responses and reactions to all sorts of things can be alarming. Apart from being negative, they can blame, appear arrogant, and be angry. However, this is a response to how they feel about themselves – and about everything. What they really mean is that they feel terrible, and lost, and that they are losing control.

Offers of help can seem patronising, even though they are given with the best of intentions. A person who is depressed desperately needs to feel that they have control over their life.

Meanwhile, the girls started their new schools, and I started a new job. We managed. We began to settle in. Jim however, did not settle. I know now how hard he was trying to keep upbeat, but underneath he was confused and agitated, and at times really tearful.

The day came to move properly – into our 'new' house. It was actually seventy years old, and needed a great deal of work. Jim had already spent some days there, dismantling the old kitchen and stripping walls. When I could, I joined him, usually supplying flasks and food. He seemed motivated, but a couple of times I'd go in to find him sitting staring into space.

"There's so much to do, I can't – I just can't do it." he said, and burst into tears. This was really worrying. Jim was a master at organisation. He could build anything, and really knew what he was doing when it came to buildings and houses. It was he who had said we should have this house, despite my reservations that it would entail a lot of work. Knowing how experienced he was, I was happy to agree. Anyway, I liked the house. His collapse like this was a shock, but I was ever-optimistic:

"Oh it's fine, we can manage for ages," I encouraged, "we've got hot water and a camping stove." Secretly I thought: "What on earth are we going to do?"

When a person is depressed they can become so overwhelmed by tasks that they are unable to see a way forward at all. To them it becomes a vast, vague 'problem'. This mindset can apply to large projects such as renovating a house, and also to mundane jobs such as washing the dishes, or even getting up and dressed. You can help your partner by encouraging them to break the job down into manageable bite-sized chunks.

What you can do to help yourself:

When everything around you seems to be falling apart, keep a sense of perspective:

- Observe others. Life goes on around you. People will still be going about their business – earning a living, doing their shopping, cooking their food and washing their clothes. They will still be laughing and crying and shouting and swearing. Seasons will come and go as usual. Flowers will grow and the birds will continue to sing.

At some stage in everyone's life they have their own challenges. But life goes on around them regardless. Somehow they come through.

- Hang on to the fact that there are thousands of people at this very moment who feel just like you do – asking themselves the same questions, and wondering what to do.

- Recognise that we can do the best that we can, but we can't control what actually happens or what other people do.

Chapter 5

The entire house needed attention. There wasn't a cupboard in sight, and the walls hadn't been painted or papered for years. Carpets and curtains had been left by the previous owners, and they were filthy. The most important thing was to create a comfortable, secure environment for the girls, who had loads to deal with emotionally – having left everything they had ever known to come here. Their new schools were enormous. They had to make new friends, and as teenagers they would have to fit in with what were already established groups and cliques. Jim and I both knew that a stable home environment would be key to helping them make that change.

My brother-in-law and a friend came to help us move, and to fit a kitchen. They and Jim worked hard together for a couple of days, and eventually it was done. The girls and I moved boxes from room to room, and there we all were – somehow – in our house, surrounded by chaos and boxes of stuff. But we now had a kitchen with cupboards and a cooker, so at least we'd be able to cook and bake and be homely.

Before he went home, I took my brother-in-law to one side.

"I'm a bit worried about Jim," I said, "he seems so down, and, well, tearful."

This was the start of a long and vital lifeline, which was to provide support and strength to both Jim and myself over the coming months. Jim's sister and

her husband offered their home as an escape for Jim at the worst times, and constant support over the phone for me.

Depression is devious. It can creep up very slowly and quietly, over a long period of time. Or it can hit like a bolt from the blue. It affects people in different ways. It is hellish for those who suffer with it, and equally hellish for those who love them and live with them – whether child, brother, sister, parent or partner.

However the relationship between partners is distinctive in that on the whole, within our western culture, partners choose each other. They want to be together. Some of the reasons they want to be together might be that they:

- love each other
- share common interests
- admire and respect each other
- find each other interesting, attractive, exciting
- give each other emotional support
- share ideas and intimacies, dreams and goals
- have great conversations
- enjoy each other's company
- have great sex together

Depression can eat away at these elements of a relationship, little by little, grinding them down to dust – just when you most need them to be there. For example:

You're worried and confused because your partner is depressed. You could do with some emotional support. Well, you're not going to get it from them, because they're ill, and because of the nature of depression – they are the centre of their universe. They need *your* support.

Maybe you need their help making crucial decisions. You probably won't get it – they're too busy being ill.

You'd like to do interesting things together. Your partner possibly has their own agenda – which may be quite different from yours.

You'd like to have sex. Maybe you will, maybe you won't.

Basically, you have to expect anything. If your partner is depressed, they are quite likely to be preoccupied with how they think and feel, which is why I said that they are 'busy being ill.' *They* take up their own time, and it's not deliberate. They can't just suddenly pull themselves out of it.

Couples adjust together and build up their lives together over a period of time. It can be challenging to accept the difference as a person changes and sinks into a depression. The changes can be very subtle, with no shift being big enough to jar you into thinking that something's not right. You may normalise anything that seems different about your partner's behaviour. You make excuses, telling yourself that there's a perfectly good explanation.

For example: "It's her time of the month…"

Or: "He's having a rough time at work at the moment…"

Maybe you don't want to acknowledge anything is wrong. There is still a stigma attached to mental illness, and if you don't know much about depression you may not want to face the fact that something really *could* be wrong. You may not want others to know about it. A mental illness can seem quite intangible and no one wants to be thought of as 'crazy' or 'mad'. Yet if your partner had any other illness – for example, cancer – would you keep that quiet?

You may blame yourself. Both males and females may feel that the responsibility for their partner's illness lies with them. You may think that you haven't provided enough, or that you have failed to meet the needs of your partner. Then the burden of guilt can be very hard to bear, even though there is probably no evidence for this at all. It may be that you deal with your feelings by denying them, or burying them. Often it takes another person to be able to face you with the changes that they see.

If you are a family member, or close friend of a couple – one of whom you suspect may be depressed – be courageous. Talk to them and their partner. Tell them (perhaps independently of each other) if things do not seem right. This may be a catalyst to get them to seek help.

If you are genuinely concerned that your partner is a danger to themselves, get in touch with someone who can help you. The Samaritans are experts in this field.

How would you know if your partner was suicidal? This is tricky, as everyone is so different. However some signs to look and listen for are:

- talking about ending their life

- getting rid of/giving away personal things

- constantly detached and withdrawn

- conversations seem to take on a strange leaning, for example: alluding to/seeming particularly excited by and interested in death

These are only *some* symptoms, so if you really feel that something is very wrong, you may just be right. *It is worth noting that research has shown that those at greater risk of attempting suicide are those who are getting better.* This is because as the lethargy they experienced in depression lifts, suicidal thoughts can remain in its place. As a person recovers, they have more energy to concentrate on these and make it happen.

www.samaritans.org Tel: 08457 909090

What you can do to help yourself:

When you feel like a limp, worn-out rag that has nothing left to give, you are no more use to your partner, your family, or yourself than a sponge. This is exactly what can happen to you in a very short space of time, as you soak up your partner's negativity, problems, anger and grumpiness. So protect yourself against this by being clear about the following:

- *You are a separate person and you have a right to your own life.* Be aware that you may need to take steps to separate yourself from your partner emotionally and psychologically. This is simply to avoid becoming 'dragged down' by their depressed state. For example, if your partner says they're lonely and they want you to stay with them, avoid saying that you'll sit with them at the cost of your own time and activities. Being there will probably make no real difference to how they feel about everything anyway. Those two or three hours, that social occasion that you could sacrifice to be with them are vital to your own well-being.

- *Be clear in your own mind about when you can talk (or be talked at) by your partner.* Jim sought me out whenever he felt like he wanted to moan. It took quite a while before I realised that by giving him that time, I was also giving the message that I was always available, and that he came first no matter what. Think carefully about this. If you don't have your own clear boundaries your energy will drain away. And if you feel guilty, you might ask yourself: "How helpful is it to feel totally exhausted when I have a family to look after and feed, and a career to maintain?"

- *Acknowledge that your partner's depression is not under your control.*

- *Avoid blaming yourself.* Be rational about this and accept that this is not your fault – even if your partner makes you think it is.

- *Take care of yourself.* You need support yourself. It may be that some counselling for yourself would be handy. I did not have this when Jim was depressed, and I am still aware of a build up of resentment over the years. You need to be able to share your thoughts and feelings, *preferably face to face with a professional.* There is no substitute for that personal contact. Being in the presence of someone who is there solely for you – being aware of their concern and understanding through their face, eyes and body language is so helpful and reassuring. If you don't see someone face to face, use the phone. The Samaritans are always there to listen, and I found this was what I needed once – just to be able to offload how I felt. MIND is a handy organisation to contact. They have a help line, and also lots of information on their website. **www.mind.org.uk** Tel: 0845 766 0163

- *Allow yourself to be happy.*

Lynne

Lynne had been with her partner for seven years:

"For the first five years Rod was very confident and ambitious, and then he lost his job. He also damaged his spine, which meant that he had to lie flat on his back for five months. The combination of those two things spiralled him into a completely different person. His identity and ego was so based around what he did in his job that when that was taken away the main building block of his self-esteem was gone. He became very withdrawn. We couldn't talk about anything – there was a complete shutdown. It is terrifying actually to see that change in someone's character. It was the disappearing into a shell, and my not being able to knock through that was the scariest thing.

While it was going on I got very down. A lot of the time I thought: "Is it me?" I started to feel that I wasn't worthy, and that he didn't love me any more. You get yourself into that spiral of "I'm terrible. I'm an awful person." I just wanted to help, but the more I tried the worse he got. He said I was pressurising him when I suggested he talk to someone. It was very distressing and it went on for such a long time. It started to become normal. I felt completely impotent. I didn't know what to do – not only for him, but for myself. I've never suffered from depression as such, but it was certainly one of the lowest points in my life. I was extremely lucky that I had a very strong group of friends around me who were really supportive.

Then he seemed to get better. He got a new job and I thought: "He's back on track now". But he never really regained his self-confidence. Outwardly, if you met him now, you'd probably think he was a very confident person, but our relationship was never the same. All the certainty had gone, including his certainty about our future. I just couldn't deal with it. It drove us apart. But it's only in retrospect that I've wondered if it was depression – I didn't really think of that at the time.

When I left, I felt as if a huge weight had been lifted. I realised that our relationship had been dying a rather slow and painful death for so long, so that I didn't feel sad. I just thought 'Thank goodness we're both out of that situation.' I had no guilt feelings at all. I just decided I'd got to get on with my own life. I'd been patient for as long as I could be and then I thought, 'Well, the only person who can get you out of this is you.'

I think as partners we have to remain positive. I'm fortunate in that I was blessed with an optimistic personality, and I'm quite independent, otherwise I think I could have gone under quickly."

Chapter 6

We were used to living in chaos. We'd totally renovated houses before, and this was nothing like that, but it was still a huge upheaval. Jim had estimated that it might take us about a year to get straight. However, neither of us had banked on the impact all this was to have on him.

Over the next few weeks things got worse and worse. Jim became more and more upset. He found even the smallest task onerous. Sometimes he just lay down – doing and saying nothing – staring at the ceiling for ages. He'd start weeping at any time of day or night, and want to talk. Well, actually, he wanted me to listen. My heart went out to him. I would have done anything to comfort the man I loved. He seemed to be in such emotional pain.

As I held him, and listened to him, I began to realise that whatever I said or suggested had little effect. He might have heard what I said, but in the depths of despair he could not listen. He was completely focused on what he was thinking and how terrible he was feeling. He went on and on, saying the same things over and over again, like a broken record:

"We should never have done it..."
"I wish we hadn't left..."
"How could we have been so stupid...?"
"Everything I ever wanted was in that house, and now it's gone..."
"I don't know what we're going to do..."
"I never thought it would come to this..."

I'd listen and try to comfort, but I felt exhausted and exasperated.

"For God's sake." I'd think. "Here we are, everything to live for, and you're like this."

One night, I thought of Aggie Armstrong. No wonder she had looked so miserable that day I returned her rose. If her Ted had been like this, she had every right to look distraught. Now I was beginning to understand why she called his 'black dog' a 'cruel bastard'.

I got hold of as much information about depression as I could. I read books and I looked for explanations. I showed them to Jim. He wasn't interested, saying that he'd look at them "later". I doubt he ever did look at them, but at least I felt a little more informed.

Depression is probably the most under diagnosed, least treated affliction of our time. It is a silent, but growing illness, a disease of the mind, body and soul that can affect anyone, at any time in their life. A great deal of research has been done into the possible causes of depression, and there are various approaches to its treatment. It is generally recognised as a serious medical condition and mood disorder, which needs to be treated, or it can last for many years.

Living the depression experience is different for everyone. The symptoms vary and it can be hellish for the sufferer, and hell for those that love them. It can hit suddenly, like a bolt out of the blue. Or it can creep up slowly, gradually seeping into every aspect of the sufferer's life, sabotaging their existence, and the lives of those around them.

The chances are that you will want to find out as much as you can about depression, and there is a vast amount of information available in books and on the internet. You could spend days trawling through everything. If you are experiencing the early stages of living with someone who is depressed, how much detail do you actually need to know? In my experience not a lot. You just need to know what you're up against and work out how you're going to cope.

Just imagine this: you are in a hardware store and you want to buy a kitchen knife, but you're not quite sure exactly which one you need. There are various types, with different names. They all have different types of blades according to the job they are meant to do. But they all have some things in common – a handle, a blade, and they are sharp. You decide to buy one general purpose knife which looks as if it will be suitable for several jobs.

Likewise, there are different types and states of depression. These have been identified by the medical profession according to the severity and type of symptoms, and on how long a person has had them. A variety of terms are used, and to the layperson this can be utterly baffling – especially when you are frantically trying to find out what the matter is with someone you care about, and how to deal with them. The Depression Alliance gives these definitions:

Reactive depression

This type of depression is triggered by a traumatic, difficult or stressful event, and people affected will feel low, anxious, irritable, an even angry. Reactive depression can also follow prolonged period of stress and can begin even after the stress is over.

Endogenous depression

Endogenous depression is not always triggered by an upsetting or stressful event. Those affected by this common form of depression will experience physical symptoms such as weight change, tiredness, sleeping problems and low mood, as well as poor concentration and low self-esteem.

I would also add that this type of depression comes from a shift or change within the person. There may be no obvious reason for it. It may be that the original stimulus lies buried deeply in their subconscious, so they are not aware of it in their conscious mind. Therefore a person knows that they feel awful but are unable to make the connection.

There are several other well-recognised forms of depression. I will discuss these later.

The main thing to realise is that all types of depression have certain things in common, and I think what you really need to know is this:

Someone who is not depressed lives from day to day experiencing a reasonable stability – a balance in their moods and mental state. There may be good moods, bad moods, highs and lows – but then everything gets back to normal. They manage their lives effectively.

When a person is depressed, this is not the case. Clinical depression is when a person's mood is generally low. It affects all aspects of their life for longer than a few weeks. Some people only have one episode of clinical depression, but for others the feelings of gloom and sadness can continue for long periods of time – months or several years. Some people are constantly depressed. Others may seem to get better, but then the depression recurs, and can recur again. Chronic depression is just this – it never really goes away.

Some people go through life almost always feeling mildly depressed. Some are unable to do anything much. Others can appear to function perfectly well in various areas of life, such as at work, but when they get home they resort to their depressed selves. The negative thoughts and feelings are always there, close to the surface. There is underlying and ongoing disease. Disease is just that, not being at ease with something in one's life. They may not be able to pinpoint exactly what it is that bothers them, but somehow, in some way, their needs are not being (or have not been) met. It may be that the reason is deeply buried somewhere in their subconscious, and something has just triggered the memory – though the person is still not aware of it. However, the thoughts and feelings that they now experience occur as a result.

The Depression Alliance lists the following most common symptoms of depression. If at least four of these persist almost *all* day, *every* day for over two weeks, then the person experiencing them is likely to be depressed:

- Tiredness and loss of energy

- Persistent sadness

- Loss of self-confidence and self-esteem

- Difficulty concentrating

- Not being able to enjoy things that are usually pleasurable or interesting

- Undue feelings of guilt or worthlessness

- Feelings of helplessness and hopelessness

- Sleeping problems – difficulties in getting off to sleep or waking up much earlier than usual

- Avoiding other people, sometimes even close friends

- Finding it hard to function at work/college/school

:: Loss of appetite

:: Loss of sex drive and/or sexual problems

:: Physical aches and pains

:: Thinking about suicide and death

:: Self-harm

www.depressionalliance.org Tel: 0845 123 2320

From my own research, I'd like to add a few more possible symptoms to the list:

:: Feelings of anxiety or emptiness
:: Feelings of inexplicable fear
:: Restlessness
:: Irritability
:: Crying a lot
:: Not being able to cry even though they feel tearful
:: Terrible feelings of guilt about something that happened long ago
:: Weight loss (due to little appetite)
:: Excessive appetite and weight gain
:: Difficulty making decisions, remembering things
:: Headaches, nausea
:: Feelings of pessimism, worthlessness, guilt
:: Increased use of alcohol and/or drugs
:: Thinking that may be going mad
:: Unpredictability
:: Completely self-absorbed
:: Sarcastic, critical, cynical
:: Pleasant in public, but foul to those that love them and live with them
:: Defensive and argumentative

What you can do to help yourself:

The best way to cope is to expect anything and everything. You are dealing with an unknown quantity here.

- Acknowledge your own feelings whilst remaining compassionate.

- Clean things and clear up. Do something to make your living environment seem bright and fresh. This may make no difference to your partner, but it will make you feel better.

It is important to make a distinction between sad or low mood states and depression. If a person feels sad or low, it generally lifts after a while. The concern is when it doesn't lift. Even when something really great happens, the depressed feelings remain and may develop.

A milder form of depression becomes a serious depression when someone's life is severely affected. The sort of things that can happen are:

- The person is likely to cut down their activities

- Things that they have enjoyed doing in the past, and friends whose company they have valued, may begin to matter less

- They may have no energy, to the extent that they can't be bothered to get out of bed, or even talk

- There is a general 'shrinking in'; that is, their outlook and horizons shrink in until there is a black hopeless and helpless core in the middle.

- It may be that the person who is depressed ceases to have an external awareness or concern about self. For example they may hold a belief such as this: "Nothing can help me. I'll never be happy again. Things are only getting worse. My own body doesn't matter so why should I bother to wash it, or feed it, or clothe it?"

∷ They may feel that there is no point in anything and that there is no way out of their own hopelessness and helplessness

They may have thoughts of and talk about suicide – *especially as they recover and their energy returns*

Anxiety

Though anxiety is not quite the same thing as depression, it is important to be aware of what it is, and the effects that it can have. Anxiety can contribute to, and occur *with* depression, therefore it is part of the same continuum. It can also go on for so long that a person feels they have lost their identity – so it actually develops into depression. It is often referred to as GAD (General Anxiety Disorder).

"The main symptom of anxiety disorder is persistent worrying, which can stop you from getting on with your life and normal daily activities. You may worry about a lot of different things at once, and feel anxious even when there's no particular reason to worry. You can't stop or control these feelings."

www.nhsdirect.nhs.uk Tel: (24 hour help line) 0845 4647.

Typically, the sort of symptoms that occur with anxiety are:

∷ Feeling very tired and vulnerable
∷ High energy at unusual times
∷ Trouble getting to sleep
∷ Waking at odd times and not being able to get back to sleep
∷ Weird and vivid dreams

:: Feeling restless, and unable to relax

:: Feeling irritable

:: Lack of concentration

:: Feeling detached and spaced out

:: Feeling tense and shaky

:: Feelings of utter and inexplicable fear

There may also be a range of physical symptoms which can be very alarming, such as:

:: Joint pains

:: Muscle pains

:: Breathlessness

:: Nausea

:: Feeling faint

:: Dizziness

:: Headaches

:: Palpitations

:: Headaches

:: Chest pains and tightness

:: Dry mouth

:: Sweating

:: Skin disorders

:: Stomach pains

:: Diarrhoea

Anxiety can lead to a range of behaviours which are similar to those in depression, and the treatment is similar.

High levels of stress can lead to anxiety. If someone becomes overwhelmed by anxiety, they could have a panic attack. This is an absolutely terrifying experience – people describe feeling as if they are having a heart attack.

Tom

Tom was a market gardener. During the Second World War he worked hard on the land. Gradually he became worried and anxious. He believed that he was going blind. The Doctor was very firm with him:

"Pull yourself together man." he told him. "You have a wife and baby to look after. There's nothing the matter with you." Somehow, this did the trick. Tom was reassured that he was well.

Current thinking does not endorse speaking to someone who is anxious or depressed in this way. When someone is falling apart in front of you, it is not usually helpful to tell them:

"Pull yourself together." or "Get a grip." or "Pull your socks up." The chances are that they can't, and they'll blame themselves because they feel that they should. This in turn will add to their feelings of anxiety or depression. However, in Tom's case, it seemed to work. Or perhaps what he really needed to hear was the reassurance that he was well.

Sophie

Sophie was twenty-four. One day she phoned her partner, almost hysterical:

"I keep feeling panicky…I'm just so scared – I don't know what's the matter with me…I had to run out of the office 'cos I felt so sick and I thought I might faint…"

She saw a doctor, who said that she may have an anxiety disorder, but first he wanted to rule out any physical causes for her symptoms.

"Understand," he told her gently and reassuringly, "that when you experience these sensations, no harm will come to you."

There was nothing physically the matter with Sophie. But her mental state was manifesting in all sorts of physical ways. She said she felt detached from things and people around her. She sometimes felt people were looking at her. She felt nauseous. Sometimes she thought she would faint. She could feel ravenously hungry, and then as soon as there was food in front of her she felt sick. She was panicky and agitated whenever she felt that she had to do something. She thought and analysed, and churned things over in her mind, especially at night. She said her dreams were weird, and she felt very tired, except sometimes late at night, when she seemed to have so much energy she felt as if she could explode.

Sophie was diagnosed as having General Anxiety Disorder, and was referred for counselling and Cognitive Behavioural Therapy. She said this helped her to manage. "But," she said, "the feelings are still there." Her ever-patient partner offered reassurance and comfort – but it was hard for him.

"I just had to trust that she would get well. My sister went through something similar, so I had some idea about it. I told her that the thoughts and feelings she had were like disruptive kids in school. They'd look for their chance and then all let rip together. I used to say that if naughty kids are ignored or not given the chance to get out of hand they'll get bored and give up. Sophie liked that. When the thoughts and feelings came flooding in, she made a point of calling them 'those kids'. It helped her to stand aside from what was happening to her a bit."

There are several other well recognised categories of depression that could affect your partner. These are:

Post-natal depression

It is important to distinguish post-natal depression from a condition called 'Baby Blues'. The latter happens shortly after giving birth, and is caused by the huge fluctuation in hormones that takes place having had a baby. 'Baby Blues' involves lots of crying, mood swings and anxiety, and usually clears up quickly.

Post-natal depression is much more serious. It may evolve from 'Baby Blues', or it may develop slowly, and the mother and others around her may not recognise it for what it is. It is horrible, and scary, and it is thought that between 10 – 30% of all women develop it in the first year after giving birth. The regular symptoms of depression may be present, and when these are coupled with other factors, for example constantly interrupted sleep, lack of help and so on, it can feel like the end of the world. A woman suffering with post natal depression needs a great deal of support. Some women have terrible experiences of post-natal depression, and this is sometimes exacerbated by medication that has been prescribed for them.

Post natal illness-support and help association:

www.pnisha.org.uk
www.apni.org Tel: 020 7386 0868

SAD (Seasonal Affective Disorder)

SAD is a type of depression that affects people over the winter months due to reduced exposure to light. This is thought to affect the chemistry in the brain. It is fairly common in the UK, and the symptoms are similar to those of depression. It is often treated by daily exposure to bright light via a special 'light box'. This can take place through hospitals, or 'light boxes' can be bought privately, which is handy as a person with SAD needs to be exposed to the light from them for between one to four hours at a time.

Studies around the world have shown that SAD becomes more common the further you are away from the equator. This suggests that SAD is linked to the change in the number of daylight hours through the year.

www.nhsdirect.nhs.uk

Other treatments are similar to those for depression, and it has also been suggested that a person who is prone to SAD will benefit from spending extra time outdoors, and from anything that helps to create an air of lightness and brightness in the environment in which they live and work.

www.sada.org.uk

Manic depression (bipolar disorder)

Manic depression is thought to be caused by a chemical imbalance in the brain, and usually medication is used to control this. It often first occurs when someone is under great stress, but this is not always the case. This is a rarer condition than other types of depression, affecting about 0.5% of the population. As with other forms, everyone's experience of it is different.

It is generally characterised by severe mood swings. There are 'up' periods of mania with huge surges of energy and activity, and sometimes irritability and anger. Then there are severe crashing 'lows' – the depression. Often this depressive phase comes first. These moods swing back and forth, for variable lengths of time. Some people only experience these occasionally, and others may have up to five or six episodes a year. If you have a partner who you suspect could have manic depression, encourage them to seek help when they are in a 'low' phase, as they are more likely to be amenable to this suggestion then.

In their information for those with manic depression, NHS direct online state:

In the depressive (low) phase symptoms may include:
- *Feeling very sad and hopeless*
- *Mental and physical slowing*
- *Lack of energy*
- *Finding it difficult to concentrate*
- *Losing interest in everyday activities*
- *Feeling of emptiness or worthlessness*
- *Feeling pessimistic about everything*
- *Feeling of serious self-doubt*
- *Difficulty sleeping, waking up early*
- *Thoughts of suicide*

The manic phase usually comes after two to four periods of depression and may include:

- *Feeling extremely happy, elated or euphoric*
- *Feeling full of energy*
- *Not feeling like sleeping*
- *Feeling full of great new ideas*
- *Feeling important*

Other people often see this differently and might think you are:

- *Speaking very quickly*
- *Changing the subject frequently*
- *Generally behaving in a strange, unusual and uninhibited way*
- *Appear unable to sit still or relax*
- *Making decisions without thinking things through*

⁚ Doing things or spending money recklessly

If you are having a manic episode, you often can't tell that anything is wrong. It can seem like other people are being critical, negative or unhelpful.

During both the manic and depressive periods of the illness you might also experience strange sensations such as seeing, hearing or smelling things that are not there (hallucinations). Or you might believe things that seem irrational to other people (delusions). This is called psychosis or a psychotic episode.

www.nhsdirect.nhs.uk

If you live with a partner who experiences manic depression, you are likely to notice some of these behaviours:

⁚ Hugely energetic
⁚ Very elated or irritable
⁚ Impulsive
⁚ Racing thoughts
⁚ Needs less sleep
⁚ Talks a lot, moves a lot
⁚ Hugely enthusiastic about what they can achieve
⁚ Euphoric about things, and change their plans frequently
⁚ Increased sexual activity
⁚ Cavalier attitude towards money
⁚ Can appear ostentatious and extravagant
⁚ Unrealistic expectations
⁚ Lows are very low and can have suicidal thoughts
⁚ Unaware of own behaviour, and feels others are critical
⁚ For some, aggression and violence

Be aware of the fact that:

When someone is in a manic phase, they are capable of sweeping everyone up in tremendous waves of enthusiasm. These waves are full of energy – everything is upbeat and can *be hard to resist.*

For example, they may expect you to drop everything immediately and *do, do, do*.

"Let's get the ferry to France...*now*." This might be a totally unrealistic proposition, but it's typically impulsive and exhausting for you if you get caught up in it. If you don't respond then and there you will probably be seen as a wet blanket, and may be criticised accordingly.

www.mdf.org.uk Tel: 08456 340 540 (UK only),
0207 793 2600 (Rest of world)

Chapter 7

When Jim was really depressed, I was exhausted. As I made the bed in the morning I longed to sink back into it again and pull the covers over my head. I craved a peaceful sanctuary and rest. At night I would fall asleep instantly, then a few hours later I'd be wide awake and agitated. I'd churn things over in my mind. I wanted answers, and I was full of self-pity and blame. I'd think things like:

"It's not fair."
"I don't know what to do"
"Perhaps I should…"
"Maybe if I'd…"
"He's so selfish."
"There's no need for this."
"I've had enough."
"I'm fed up."
"Why's this happening?"
"What have I done wrong?"
"How could I have done things differently?"
"What has he done to deserve this?"

I spent hours and hours going over things. I was preoccupied most of the time with thoughts such as these, until I did something about it.

Why it's important to keep positive

Language is your most powerful tool. The way that you communicate with yourself and with others has an impact on how you think, feel and behave. Therefore it is a fundamental part of your life, and the lives of those around you.

Your 'self-talk' – what you tell yourself in your head is very important, as it can reinforce itself, and the effect it can have on you. So it's important to understand something of how the mind works. Then you can make your self-talk work for you.

Basically there are two parts to the mind, the conscious and the subconscious.

Your conscious mind:

You are aware and in the present with your conscious mind. This is the reasoning part of your mind – the part that makes decisions and choices. It acts as a filter to thoughts and suggestions, deciding where to place them or whether to get rid of them. When a thought or suggestion is accepted, the information filters into the subconscious.

Your subconscious mind:

The subconscious then organises the information. It's a container for your thoughts and feelings. It is amazing, and it works incredibly hard. This is the part of the mind that deals with all the automatic workings of your body, such as your heartbeat and your breathing, so it works whilst you are awake and asleep. It never stops.

The subconscious takes orders from the conscious mind. It is extremely obedient and believes that what it is told is true. It doesn't discriminate, and it has absolutely no sense of humour.

Once the subconscious accepts an idea it starts to implement it. It doesn't care whether it is a good or a bad idea – it's only interested in obeying what the conscious has told it to do. Then the really hard work starts. The subconscious makes sure that the suggestion or idea is carried out, and it creates the right conditions for this to happen.

For example, if you have constantly negative thoughts, and you repeat them often enough, they will filter into your subconscious. It will accept these as the truth. It will then create an environment where these can take over. Similarly, when your thoughts are repeatedly positive *and you really believe them*, your subconscious works to make sure that these flourish and you thrive.

Imagine that as an experiment you plant two saplings side by side. You give the first one fertiliser from a packet called 'Doom and Gloom.' This is full of poison. You give the other sapling 'Bright and Optimistic' fertiliser, which you know is really beneficial. The fertilisers filter through the top layers of soil down to where the saplings' roots are. Every now and then you top up their water with a little more fertiliser from their corresponding packets.

In the fullness of time you go to look at the trees, and guess what? The tree that was fertilised with 'Doom and Gloom' is withered and gnarled. Its branches have shrivelled and twisted. The ground around it is bare and dry.

The tree that was fed with 'Bright and Optimistic' has really grown. Its branches are strong and far-reaching. It is covered in healthy green leaves. People gravitate towards it because it attracts them, and it is a good place to be.

You decide to help the withered tree, and start feeding it with 'Bright and Optimistic'. After a short time you notice that the tree is more upright. Its branches are straightening out, and they are stronger. As time goes on it becomes more and more like the other tree. Now it too, is a good place to be. At any point you can save the withered tree by feeding it with good fertiliser.

At any point you can change your thinking by feeding your mind with positive self-talk, and replacing negative thoughts with positive ones. It's really important that you do this, and that you fully believe those thoughts. This will help you to keep upbeat, and make you more resilient to the effect of your partner's negativity.

What you can do to help yourself:

- Breathe deeply and *smile*. Take a moment to breathe in deeply, right into your abdomen. (If your shoulders go up, you are only breathing into the top part of your lungs, so you want to take a good deep breath). As you breathe out, lift your body upright and really smile. Say to yourself mentally or out loud: "I'm OK, I can cope with this." *And believe it.*

- Do this whenever you remember – do it often enough and it will become automatic. It's a good habit to get into, because it will lift your energy.

Chapter 8

We never knew what would happen when we opened the front door and stepped into our house. Often the girls would come home from school to find Jim in tears, or in bed.

"I don't know what the matter is," he'd tell them piteously. "I'm sorry. I don't know *what* to do." It was awful for them, and they didn't really know what to do for the best. When I came home, I had the same treatment. Any of us might be sitting watching TV, and he could appear at the door – desperate, shaking his head and saying "It's all gone wrong", "I just don't know what to do…" and then retreat back into the other room. Sometimes he'd come and sit with us, putting an enormous dampener on everything. His misery and negativity filled the room.

At some point I remember saying to him privately that it wasn't fair to talk to the girls like this, and that it was upsetting for them. I suggested he talk to me about how he was feeling instead. He agreed. He talked to (or at) me about his feelings all the time anyway. Though Jim made a concerted effort to curb his moroseness in front of the girls, it was short-lived. He just couldn't seem to help himself. He wondered around the house like a lost soul – feeling dreadful and needing to express himself somehow, to anybody, whenever he felt he needed to.

What you can do to help yourself:

- Envisage your protective invisible bubble around you as often as you can. Some people feel a protective bubble around themselves physically, whilst others imagine they see it. One person I worked with used to hear it vibrating at a very low frequency. I used to imagine a golden bubble around me before I went inside the house – where I knew Jim would be.

Jim knew that something was wrong. He must have felt very confused and frightened at this time. I remember suggesting that he should get some help, and this is something that he did quite willingly. I was fortunate that he was prepared to do this. Not everyone is.

It is vital that your partner visits a doctor in the first instance, to eliminate any physical reasons for the way they feel. Some medications can have side effects of depression, as can some illnesses and infections.

If they won't go – you do it! It's worth having a discussion with your GP and voicing your concerns. They may well be able to advise you as to the next step you can take.

If your partner is refusing to see the doctor, you may be able to coax them gently. It's worth planning how you are going to do this, because if you are confrontational, you will probably hit a brick wall. Ultimately it is up to your partner to take the decision to seek help, but you can have an input. By stealth, you can enable them to take this step – through the way that you talk to them. Here are some ideas:

Gently state your concern about how your partner's mood is affecting them, and its impact on you (and the family). You could say that you're also concerned that it could be due to something physical, so they need to get checked out. *Be gentle and motivational.* For example:

"I hate to see you so unhappy at the moment, and we all want you to be fine

again. I'm just wondering if there could be any reasons we haven't thought of, and how it might be helpful to get checked out. It would be great to be clear wouldn't it — so that we can move forward?"

This may sound extraordinary when you read it, and it may not be appropriate for you, so be creative. The main thing is to be supportive and motivational. Avoid referring to your partner as "you" too often, or it will sound accusatory. For example: "You're obviously ill and you need to get to the doctor."

Another way to approach the topic is to be genuinely inquisitive. Useful phrases might be:

"I'm just wondering what/if…"

"I wonder how things might improve if you were to (get help)…"

"I wonder how we could all benefit from…"

You could act confused and ask for your partner's help to understand. Like this:

"It sounds like on the one hand you're (really unhappy), and on the other hand (you don't want to get any help). I'm just a bit confused — I don't quite understand what your thinking behind that is…can you help me out…?"

It may be worth agreeing with them when they say there is no need for help:

"Maybe you're right and there's nothing to be concerned about. I'm just wondering if it would be useful to have more information so that we can know for sure…"

It's important that your partner realises that it is not them but their behaviour that is the concern, and that you want them to get help because you care about them. By your tactful 'chipping away' they may come to realise that they have to do something about it.

If you still aren't getting anywhere, is there anyone else that you could ask to have a word with them, such as a good friend or family member? If your partner realises that others have seen a change in them, they might listen to them.

Throughout all this, your partner needs to hear what their strengths are. They may not believe that they have any, so they need you to tell them. By doing this you are feeding their subconscious with positive messages.

John

John's partner said:

"John had felt really low for weeks. There seemed to be no particular reason – he was just fed up. He'd gone off his food, and I was worried about him. He'd get in from work each night and sit down with a couple of cans in front of the TV. He'd hardly speak to me at all. Well, he agreed to see the doctor, and I went with him. It was good to be able to share my concerns. But John thought it was a waste of time. The doctor asked us a few questions and examined him, but she said she wasn't entirely sure what was the matter. She told him to take things easy and to go back in a couple of weeks if he still felt the same. He felt really fed up then. He just thought he'd been 'fobbed off'.

He didn't get any better and we went back. This time the doctor said he had depression and gave him a prescription. At least he felt he was being taken seriously then."

Hannah

Hannah, a student, went to see the university GP. She suspected she might be depressed. She explained her symptoms and asked for a blood test just to make sure there was nothing physically wrong. The doctor was very abrupt with her and told her that she didn't need a blood test. Hannah felt anxious, worried and foolish when she left the surgery.

After a week she returned, accompanied by her mother. This time she saw a different doctor. Hannah was given a thorough medical examination and her blood was tested for a variety of different illnesses and deficiencies. This gave her great reassurance that she was being taken seriously. A few days later, the results of her tests showed that physically Hannah was fine. The doctor diagnosed an anxiety disorder, and discussed the treatment options with Hannah.

It's important to realise that:

Doctors have guidelines which help to provide a diagnostic tool when deciding whether or not someone is depressed. If in the course of seeing a person and hearing what they have to say, they decide that they do not meet these, then they may see no need for further action at that point.

It may be that by returning after a week or two the patient does meet these criteria, and the response may be quite different.

When another person who is close to the depressed person sees the doctor with them, it can make a difference. They may remember symptoms and behaviours that have been forgotten. Also, another person's concern is unlikely to go unnoticed.

Doctors are incredibly busy people, and they have a vast amount of knowledge. As with all of us, some are better at interpersonal communication skills than others.

Chapter 9

It must have been so miserable for Jim. He felt desperate. He was overwhelmed by his thoughts and feelings. So it was amazing that he was able to see how awful it was for us to have him around. At least I think that's what he thought. On the other hand he may have just needed to escape.

He did frequently go away. He stayed with his sister, Trish, and her husband who were a fantastic support to us both. I was really grateful for this, as it gave us all a break. At least while he was away there was an air of stability in the house.

If he was away over a weekend, I did some decorating. It was quite a boost to do something practical. It provided a respite from the worry, and it was great to see rooms looking light and bright again. One day I spoke to Jim on the phone.

"How's things?"

"All right." he said sounding unusually cheerful.

"I was wondering," I said, "d'you reckon the girls and I might go and get some carpet?"

"Yeah, see what you can find. Good idea." We exchanged some strangely uncharacteristic pleasantries, and he chuckled. I was surprised by his tone of voice and manner. He sounded fine.

Partners who are depressed and angry can be perfectly pleasant in public.

When they return to you they can be horrible, manipulative, nasty and cruel.

Partners who are depressed can also be foul to you in public.

Jim spoke abruptly to me sometimes, and this was noticed and commented on by others sometimes.

Partners who are depressed can, if they feel so inclined, bitch about you to others when you are not there.

Sometimes when Jim stayed with Trish he told her how awful I was, and how everything was my fault. He repeated this over and over again. I know this, because Trish told me. I'm sure he spoke about me in this way to other people too.

When Jim returned, we had samples of carpet for him to inspect. We were upbeat and excited. Perhaps this would please him. Maybe he was feeling better – after all, he'd sounded quite cheerful. But Jim was not feeling cheerful. He was just as miserable as he'd been before he'd left. The atmosphere in the house returned to one of gloom and unease. The carpet samples we'd collected were stuffed in a bag and left there. We tried to help him drum up some enthusiasm:

"Dad – how about this?" or "I like that colour. What d'you think?"

"Do what you want." he said, making a huge effort to smile.

"Yes, but Dad, what do *you* want?"

"Anything," he sighed. "I don't care." Jim's sense of hopelessness had taken over.

Roz

Mary's world was very rosy – she had work she enjoyed, and she and her partner were expecting a baby. Sometimes her colleague Roz would come in, do some work, and then have to leave the room. When she returned, it was evident that she'd been crying. If anyone asked if she was all right, she'd say, "Yes, it's nothing."

One day, as soon as Roz arrived at work, she burst into tears. She explained that her husband was depressed.

"It's so awful," she said. "I don't know what to do. The children are sick of it. It just seems endless. Every day, more misery. He's so negative all the time…"

Roz's husband was in his late fifties and had been made redundant. It had hit him hard. Their children were grown up, but were clearly affected by his depression. Mary said:

"One day Roz asked a few of us to lunch. To be honest, I didn't know anything about depression. We had a lovely meal, and Roz seemed quite happy. Her husband was amiable and friendly towards us, and was a great host. I couldn't really understand how this charming man could be causing her so much grief. He seemed a genuinely lovely person, and I couldn't equate him with depression and misery at all."

Several years later, Mary's husband became depressed – which is when I met her. It was then that she told me about Roz, and how at that time she'd been baffled by her situation, as she hadn't really understood it.

"Well, I can really understand now." she said. "I know just what it must have been like for Roz at that time."

What you can do to help yourself:

Living with a partner who is depressed creates stress for you. This needs to be released somehow.

How do you relax? You might like to:

- Flop in front of the TV or go to a movie
- Quietly read a book
- Do a jigsaw
- Do physical exercise
- Enjoy a meal or a drink
- Take a long, hot bath

The list is endless, and it's really important to do something that you like doing, that is just for you.

Another excellent way of concentrating exclusively on yourself is to spend some time quietly relaxing your body. Once you have got the hang of this, the rewards and benefits are terrific. It centres and strengthens you mentally, and it rejuvenates you physically. It increases your awareness of your own body, which helps you to recognise when you are misplacing energy and becoming tense.

When I was about ten years old, our teacher used to march us into the school hall and make us lie down.

"Silently." she ordered. "I want to be able to hear a pin drop."

"Why does she want to hear a pin drop?" I thought.

"A *pin* drop." she reiterated as we settled down. Some of us tittered and giggled and tried to distract each other.

"I'm waiting." she persisted. Eventually it became quiet.

"Now close your eyes." Then she began to speak very quietly:

"Listen to the sounds outside the room. Don't say anything, but just be aware of them." Then after a minute or two she said:

"Now bring your attention into the building, and just listen. Listen to the sounds *inside* the building." What a great way of getting us to focus our attention that was. It always worked. We were so focused and quiet, she could probably have heard that pin drop. Next she went on:

"Now turn your attention to your own body. Be aware of your feet. Be aware of your toes. Give them a little stretch, and then let them go. Just let them go. And then your calves. Let them feel heavy and floppy…" and she continued directing us to relax every bit of our body in turn so that we felt heavy, as if we were sinking into the floor.

Our shoulders became broad and wide, and she paid great attention to our heads and faces – back of head, top of head, forehead, eyelids, cheeks, jaw, lips, tongue…it seemed as if no piece of our bodies escaped.

When we were all like lumps of lead, she waited a minute, then told us to turn on one side and curl up.

"Now *very slowly, in your own time*, sit up and gently open your eyes." Then she told us that a few minutes of deep relaxation is as good as an hour's sleep. She also said that the more we did it, the more we would get used to it, and then we'd be able to do it anywhere – on a bus, on a train perhaps. Without a doubt, that was one of the finest things I ever learnt in school. It has stood me in good stead all my life.

You may be used to doing this already, especially if you do an activity such as yoga. If it is new to you, you might like to give it a try. Learning to relax your body can take time and effort.

You may find that your mind races, and that your body twitches. That's OK, it gets easier.

There are many recorded relaxation tapes and CDs available. You may like to try one. Be sure however that it does a progressive relaxation of your body. Alternatively, try the method below. You could record yourself, or ask someone to read it. But I reckon if you read it through a couple of times first you'll be ready to have a go. You need about fifteen to twenty minutes, and to be quiet and undisturbed, and you need to be comfortable and warm:

- Lie down or sit in a chair.

- Close your eyes. This is important, as it frees you from extra distractions.

- Listen to the sounds around you. Just be aware of the myriad sounds in your environment – outside then inside the building, the sounds of your own body and your breathing.

- Take your attention to each part of your body, *slowly* tensing and then relaxing each in turn. Start with your toes, then feet, ankles, lower legs, upper legs, buttocks, torso, fingers, arms, shoulders, neck, back of head, top of head, forehead, eyelids, cheeks, nose, jaw, and tongue.

- Tense each part – and let it go. Let each part of your body flop and relax. Take your time, there's no rush.

- Let your breath flow gently in and out of your body.

- Eventually you will become relaxed and still.

- You might like to go a stage further and imagine yourself in a beautiful and relaxing place. Stay there for a few minutes.

- When you are ready, stretch and open your eyes. Allow yourself to come round *slowly*.

- *Slowly* sit up (if you are lying down). Keep in the moment – let the relaxed feeling stay with you for as long as you can.

It doesn't really matter how you learn to relax, as long as you build up an awareness of the sensations. Systematically tensing and relaxing your muscles is a great way, as it helps to increase you own body awareness.

Once you have done this a few times you will find that you can become relaxed quite quickly, in all sorts of situations, such as when you're sitting at your desk, or doing the washing up. Be aware of unnecessary tension in your body. Tell yourself to relax and let go. We often carry a load of tension in our shoulders and neck, so remember to tense and release these regularly throughout the day.

It is thought that approximately one in four people experience anxiety or depression of some kind in the course of their lives. Although statistics provide a useful guide, they are always slightly out of date, due to the time it takes to collect and translate them. Other factors to consider are:

People do not always ask for help. This may be due to a lack of knowledge about depression – the symptoms and treatments available. It may also be due to the stigma that still surrounds mental illness.

Sometimes depression is wrongly diagnosed.

Therefore, many people are likely to be walking around undetected, undiagnosed and untreated.

Anyone can experience depression regardless of age or culture, therefore men, women and children are affected. It is now thought to occur as often in men as in women, irrespective of age.

The experience of depression may be different for men and women, for all sorts of reasons. Here are a few:

- Some men don't talk about their feelings

- Some men are not as willing to get help as women generally are

- Some men prefer to think they can cope with their depression themselves

- In general, women tend to turn to others for support

- Women tend to be more at ease talking about feelings

So why does depression occur?

This is the subject of much debate, and it seems that any of the following reasons, or a combination of several can cause depression:

Health – it can occur because of an illness or medical condition. It can also be a symptom of an infection. Research shows that nutrition affects mental health.

Drugs – it can come about as a result of substance abuse. It can also be a side effect of some medications.

Genetic – if there is a family history of depression, a person may be more vulnerable to becoming depressed themselves.

Biological – a change can occur in the chemicals in the brain which therefore affects a person's thoughts and feelings.

Psychological – a person may have certain characteristics that could mean they are more likely to become depressed. For example: low self-esteem, a generally pessimistic outlook on life, a sense that they have no control over their life, worrying excessively about things, being unable to cope adequately with difficult situations or stress.

Environmental

Things that happen in a person's life can contribute to depression. Examples of these may be: conflict, loss (perhaps of a job or a relationship), bereavement, lack of support, a trauma.

The depression itself can be the reason why some of these things happen.

For example: a person is depressed and so they are no fun to be around. Therefore their partner gets fed up and leaves. The depressed person feels the loss and becomes even more depressed.

The effects of loss

Much depression does seem to be to do with loss of some kind, and it can often be loss of identity due to various factors. These can be loss of:

faculties
physicality
relationship
job
finance/house

The effects of loss can be far reaching. For example, a job or career might have provided an opportunity for a person to express a certain part of themselves. When that is removed, there may seem to no longer be an outlet for this. So this need to express turns inwards… and if left too long can fester and contribute to depression.

Conflict and repressed emotions

Similarly, repressed emotions can have a devastating effect. For example, if someone is angry and frustrated with a person, but feels they are not allowed to be, the emotions can turn inwards where they can become self-attack. As an example, if a child has been abused by a parent, they may feel that they can't be angry with them. The dis-ease they experience as a result may show as low self-esteem. Eventually this may grow into self-neglect or self-harm. It's as if that person is saying "I can't be angry with you, so I must deserve this. I'll show you what you made me do."

Trauma

There is no doubt that some depression occurs as a result of an event, which the person found unduly stressful or traumatic. For example, a bereavement or the loss of a job. The depression may not begin until after the event is over.

Sometimes the memory of a trauma has lain dormant for years, and then it is triggered by something and the depression kicks in. For example, it is quite common for the memory of an event which happened in childhood to be filed away in the subconscious, only to resurface in adulthood when something 'gives it a nudge'.

To sum up, the majority of depression occurs because something is not 'right' with that person. There is dis-ease within – some sort of needs are not being met. The sufferer may not know the cause, and they may not ever need to. This depends on the person and the treatment they seek.

But a person who is depressed needs help, and if it's someone you live with and love – so do you.

Chapter 10

When Jim was diagnosed with clinical depression, I thought things might get better. He had appointments with a psychiatrist and a counsellor. I hadn't thought for one moment that things might actually get worse. Everything prior to this had just been the preamble to a hideous time, when I was to question whether I would leave, and uproot our daughters yet again.

Jim was prescribed medication, which I uncharacteristically encouraged him to take. I am a strong advocate of homeopathy, and I know that it can be particularly useful when someone is depressed. However, as we had just moved, we hadn't found a homeopath, and anyway, Jim's first port of call is always to the doctor if something is wrong. But he was against taking medication, and flushed some of it down the toilet. He obviously realised that something had to be done though, because it didn't take long before he was taking his daily dosage quite rigorously.

Much later, in a sudden outburst, Jim was to accuse me of turning him into a "Bloody junkie." Around that time he weaned himself off the medication. This worked for him – but it is not advisable. It is supposed to be supervised by a doctor.

I'm not sure what difference the medication made. Perhaps it helped him to be a little calmer. I had no idea what he was prescribed, or when he took it. If he'd wanted me to know, he'd have told me.

How you may be able to help your partner

These points may be useful for you to keep in mind. I didn't always – and I wish I had.

Make sure your partner knows you are there for them, and that you care about them.

Keep a clear sense of your own boundaries and let them know this. For example, they may phone you with some trauma when it is really inconvenient for you – maybe you're at work. Tell them when you can take a call, or deal with their texts, or when you are able to talk to them. You need to be clear about your own boundaries, because theirs will be non-existent.

Realise that if your partner is depressed, they will be spending most of their time thinking about how they feel. Whether or not what they do is convenient for you will probably never enter their head. Help them by giving them a structure.

Help your partner to make clear and realistic goals, which will maintain their sense of responsibility. Large tasks can seem really daunting to someone who is depressed, so encourage them to break them down into small, achievable ones. *When someone is really depressed, even the most mundane task can seem like an insurmountable problem. Expect that they may not achieve what you both planned – but don't let them know that. Respect the fact that they have even thought about it, and say something genuinely positive by way of encouragement.*

Avoid giving your partner excuses for their behaviour. Avoid helping them to find easy ways out. If you do this they have your permission to carry on as they are, and to see their self as an invalid and a victim.

Avoid patronising your partner and treating them like a child. This can be easier said than done when you feel frustrated and desperate yourself. You may think you know best (and it may be that you do), but you will only increase their feelings of powerlessness.

Though they feel desperate, they need to retain a sense of responsibility for their life.

Avoid saying "Don't worry." Most people hear the main verb and latch on to it. So if you say "Don't worry", they hear *"Worry."*

You could change the emphasis by saying:

"I can see that you *might* be worried, *but* (you're able to get through this)."

Using 'but' is handy here as it enables you to acknowledge their feelings and then add something positive.

Alice

Alice's mother, in her mid fifties, had suffered from depression and General Anxiety Disorder for two years. Hypnotherapy had unearthed the forgotten trauma of childhood abuse, which was at the root of her distress. However, she still had some way to go in order to recover, and though medication seemed to help, she tended to phone Alice whenever she felt particularly low or panicky. Alice would just have to listen, and try to calm her. There was not much else she could do. Later, her mother would phone in floods of tears to apologise for being such a nuisance.

Understandably Alice was very worried. Sometimes she looked as if she was fighting back the tears:

"It's so wearing," she told me. "I try to sound positive, but she doesn't hear that. All she can think about is how she feels. She just goes over and over the same things — she can't seem to get out of this negativity..."

I asked her how her mother's partner coped. Alice shook her head.

"He doesn't really. He just gets frustrated. It's hard for him, but he can't empathise. They're meant to be going on holiday, but I don't know if mum will be able to — she panics so much whenever she thinks about it. But he gets so wound up by it. He just says things like, 'If you won't go, I'll go without you.' He doesn't realise how unhelpful this is."

A depressed person can become so focused on their negative thoughts and feelings, that it becomes their normal mood state. They can't seem to break this. To them, everything has a down side — as if they are stuck in an ever-shrinking, oppressive mental black box.

You want to help and to understand them. So you listen intently to them. But beware: you may find that you get so caught up in what they say that you're almost sucked into their black box with them. If you are emotionally involved with that person, and if you have a history together, this is far more likely to happen because you want to help them so much. You almost want to be able to feel their pain. But, actually, how useful is this to them, or to you?

You need to be compassionate, and to be empathic. But there is little point in you sharing their suffering. You need to think of yourself as a separate package — a professional, a therapist for them. No matter how intimately involved you are with someone — once they have become depressed, you will have to shift the boundaries if you are to survive. Ultimately you want them to put the lid on their black box. You don't need to climb in there with them.

So in order to avoid being lulled into your depressed partner's despondency, you could try these:

Notice your own tone of voice

Be empathic, but keep your voice upbeat and fairly 'matter-of-fact'. When you sound really empathic, and when you say kindly: "I know, it must be awful." Or "Mmm, I see what you mean." too many times, it encourages the person to say more. The only thing is that they are likely to say more of the same thing, over and over again. This prolongs their negative mood state, and slowly sucks you into it along the way.

Notice the words they use, and when they are negative encourage them to challenge what they say

This way, they challenge their negative thoughts, and you help them to break their mood state because you distract them. Very often when people are depressed they tend to make sweeping statements. They refer to "everything" and "all", and use broad general terms. You can challenge these by getting them to be more specific. (They probably won't like you for it, as it is breaking their chain of thought – but this is what you are after.)

They say:	You reply:
It's no good.	*What's* no good?
I'm fed up.	What are you fed up *about*?
My life is shit.	*How* is your life shit?
Bad things always happen.	*Always?* *How* are they bad? *When* do they happen *exactly*?
I can't do anything right.	*What* is it that you can't do?
Everything's going wrong.	*What's* going wrong the most?
No one cares.	*No one?*

	Who specifically doesn't care?
It's a waste of time.	*What exactly* is it that's a waste of time? *How?*
I can't face it.	*What is it* that you can't face? *Which bit?*
Nothing ever works.	Nothing at all? Ever? *What is it* that doesn't work?
I feel bad.	*How* do you feel bad? *Where* in your body?
It's all too much!	*What* is?

So what you're doing is questioning general statements like: 'always', 'never', 'nobody', 'everybody', by asking for evidence, and getting them to be specific.

Avoid asking them closed questions like:

"can you?"
"do you?"
"is it?"
"was it?"
"did it?"

As these only need "yes" or "no" for an answer. The depressed person may shut up for a while, but then they'll start up again and you won't have got very far.

You may already be familiar with this type of questioning. However, if you are not, it may seem daunting – especially when you are in the middle of an emotional situation.

All it needs is practice, and then you'll find that you get into the swing of it.

If this is new to you, I suggest that the best thing to do is to identify a couple of general sweeping statements that your partner uses quite often. Work out how to challenge these in the manner that I've shown, and then have a go. See what happens. You are unlikely to lose out. It just breaks the negative patterns – even if only momentarily. This will prevent you from getting lulled into despondency too, as well as helping them by breaking their thought patterns.

A word of warning: Avoid overdoing this type of questioning or you can sound as if you are interrogating.

Here's a couple more ideas:

When your depressed partner makes the piteously general statement: *I just can't.*
you could ask:
What would happen if you could?

or:
Just suppose you could – what would that be like?

Something else that can pull a person up in their tracks is for you to act confused. You could say:

"I'm sorry – I'm not sure what you mean. Could you explain this to me again?"

Though they may not like it, they have to stop to answer you. Also, this gives them a chance to see if what they said is really what they meant. They'll have to elaborate on what they said or explain it differently, or just give up. Either way, their negative mood state will have been temporarily broken, and you'll be standing your ground.

Chapter 11

Then it just happened. There was a tumultuous shift. I don't remember how or when it came about, but it was far worse to deal with than anything that had gone before. Jim's tears stopped. So did his sorrow and lethargy, moping and pouting. Instead he was angry. He became like a smouldering volcano, whose rage and hatred bubbled under the surface until it erupted in a passionate rage. He would seek me out, wherever I was, whatever I was doing, to hurl all sorts of crazy accusations and expletives my way:

"It's all down to you, you manipulated me. You made us move to this poxy place. You're so selfish - you had it planned all along. You never cared about anybody but yourself – so long as you get what you want, you don't care."

It seemed as if he would burst if he didn't say everything all at once. It was as if he had some sort of hideous verbal diarrhoea which had to be expelled the moment he was aware of it. Physical diarrhoea can usually be cleared up. Verbal diarrhoea, when it is negative and accusatory, and aimed at you, is much trickier to get rid of. The effects linger and taint everything you do.

Each verbal attack is like twisting a knife in an emotional wound. The effect can mount up, and grind you down. So can constant exposure to negativity. You experience so many emotions, not least of which are resentment, anger, sadness and hurt. The thing that may not be obvious at first is that both you and your partner may be experiencing similar emotions – but for different reasons.

Your partner probably feels they are doing their best to deal with how they are experiencing their depression, and they may well feel that you don't understand. You also may feel that you are trying your best. But how can you give love and support when you are attacked so much, or when you feel you have nothing left to give?

As this continues, you are likely to withdraw from each other, because neither of you is getting what you need. You can't seem to sort things out and everything gets worse.

So take steps to protect yourself, so that your emotional wounds have a chance to heal.

What you can do to help yourself:

Recognise that you may have no control over what has happened, or over your partner's behaviour. But you do have a choice about how you deal with your own thoughts and feelings.

One thing I found useful when things were particularly bad was this:

I made a spider diagram. In the centre was 'Jim's depression'. This was useful as a focus, and it consolidated the fact in my own mind that it was his *behaviour*, not *him*, that was at the centre of this.

From this central point I wrote down all my thoughts and feelings, and added to them every now and then – things like: "angry", "desperate", "I can't stand this". After a while, there was nothing more to add – the same thoughts and feelings kept coming up.

> One morning I woke up in the early hours, and felt strangely clear-headed and determined. I picked up the diagram. Before each statement I wrote 'I choose to feel…' or 'I have decided that…'
>
> This was amazingly powerful. I realised then that I was not a victim in all this. I had some control.

Jim's behaviour had changed. It was, well – unexpected and bewildering. Quite often he seemed to have abnormal reactions to 'normal' situations. For example, he spent the majority of the time in one room. Sometimes, I assumed we might be disturbing him, and pulled the door to. Suddenly, he would appear with a look of utter shock on his face, like a rabbit startled in headlights.

"Is something happening?" he'd ask suspiciously as he looked around. "You shut me in. Why did you shut me in?"

It took me a while to realise that what he may well have meant was:

"I'm here. I'm ill. I'm confused. Help me."

For a while, Jim became very sensitive to noises – and made sure we knew. If we unintentionally made any noise, he came out of the room and banged the door shut, loudly enough to register his irritation. But if it was he who made the noise, then it became my fault. For example, if he had the TV volume louder than normal, and I dared to ask him to turn it down, I quickly wished I hadn't bothered. The very fact that I had asked triggered a tirade of verbal abuse and bad language. The 'black dog' had really got Jim now. It was constantly ready to pounce.

I couldn't go into our tiny kitchen if Jim was in there. He'd sigh, roll his eyes, slam down a cup or something and say there wasn't room. Surely I could wait until he'd finished? Yet the girls and I were frequently in the kitchen at the same time. We just managed to work round each other.

What you can do to help yourself:

If you're feeling particularly wound up you might:

Count down from twenty to one. This works better that counting up from one to twenty, as you'll find that counting *down* calms you down. Imagine each number as you do so. This will help you to focus.

Whilst you listen to your partner being irrational, or accusing you, or repeatedly being negative, mentally say to them: "This is your issue – not mine." Repeat this as often as you need to. Develop the skill so that you are able to do it while you are talking to them as well.

This may seem unkind, but it allows you to distance yourself slightly, and helps their negativity to bounce off you instead of being absorbed.

Chapter 12

Jim usually cut the grass, but occasionally I did it. When he was ill I thought it would please him if he found the job done. It didn't. He told me in no uncertain terms that I hadn't cut it correctly. It was "Uneven".

He no longer ate the food I cooked. He'd toy with what was on his plate, and then almost retch as he raised the fork to his lips. It was "Too chompy." He went off certain ingredients, and always acted as if I'd purposely included them just to annoy him.

"You know I don't like carrots."

"Well," I'd say, "could you pick them out? Just leave them." But he'd sigh and slam down his fork.

"I can't eat this." And the food would be left on the plate. An hour or two later he'd poach himself an egg.

I had absolutely no idea what to do for the best. It was as if I'd swapped a partner for a bolshie teenager. Later I'd hear him talking to someone on the phone. He'd be charming and witty – a far cry from the belligerent individual that I was learning to live with.

If you think your partner is becoming depressed, notice three things:

Posture
When they stand, are they upright or do they slouch? Is this more or less than it used to be, or about the same? How do they sit? What

messages do you get from their body language? Does it seem easy and comfortable, or do they seem tense and protective of themselves? For example, their legs may be crossed and their arms folded.

Notice this, because there may be some change

Movement

How does your partner walk and move? Do they walk more slowly than usual? Where do they place their head, and where do they look? For example, is it downwards? Or do they walk quickly, and pace the floor? Is it more or less than it used to be, or about the same?

Just notice, and be aware of any change.

Voice

How does your partner sound? Happy? Fed up? Agitated? Is their voice louder or quieter than it used to be? Does it sound flatter or sharper than usual? Do they talk on one note all the time – if so, is this more or less than it used to be? Does their voice go down at the end of each sentence?

Just notice, and be aware of change.

It can be tricky to notice subtle differences in someone's demeanour when you are emotionally involved and know them very well, but there will be changes though they may not be obvious at the time. The reason for the change is that the depressed person's energy will shift. They will focus their time, energy and attention on the way that they think and feel. This will generally lead them downward and inward.

If your partner has manic depression, their energy during their mania phases will be boundless. They will talk quickly with huge enthusiasm, and this will be reflected by the energy in their movement and posture.

In the build up to Jim's depressed state, I suppose I did notice changes, but as I had no idea that he was actually becoming depressed, I paid little attention. It was only when he was diagnosed that I really made the link between the changes in his demeanour and voice and how he felt.

For example, on the rare occasions when we ate together, he sat sideways on his chair with one leg crossed over the other by the side of the table. So his body looked twisted, like a corkscrew. I was sure he had not sat like this before, and for some reason I found it infuriating.

"Why does he do that?" I'd think. If he'd been a child I'd probably have told him to "sit properly." But I never mentioned it, and I doubt whether Jim even noticed that he did it. I reckon that maybe he felt less vulnerable sitting in this way. When he finished eating, he always folded his arms across his chest. So the picture was complete – closed, protective body language. As time went on, I felt that his physical demeanour was so closed, protective and taught that he could just snap.

Jim sounded noticeably different too. A lot of the time his voice was a monotone, and he spoke more quietly than he used to, so that I constantly had to ask him to repeat what he said. That is, unless he was lecturing me in a loud purposeful voice, or yelling at me.

He often rolled his eyes to the ceiling and sighed. These were huge sighs that seemed to ripple right through his body – usually when I asked him something, or disturbed his thoughts in some way.

So what did all this tell me? It told me that the man that I had lived with for years had changed. That he was not at ease with himself or the world around him, and that he needed help. It told me that he was likely to be resistant to anything I suggested, so I should beware and tread carefully.

My daughter had a friend called Emma, who was friendly and fun when she was at school. I used to enjoy the occasional chats we had. They left school and I didn't see her for a year or so. Then one day she rang up to speak to my daughter. I asked her how she was and I was shocked at how different she sounded:

"Oh, you know – all right…" she sounded exhausted and, well, dreary. Apparently she had become depressed – and she sounded it. When I saw her, she didn't look any different from a year previously. She carried herself in the same manner – upright, slow and steady. But the tone of her voice spoke volumes.

What you can do to help yourself:

Always remember that you may not be able to change a situation, but you can change the way you manage your own feelings about it.

When you live with someone who is depressed, you can feel an eclectic mixture of emotions at any given time. It may seem as if you are on an emotional roller coaster, or you may feel as if you are living in an emotional fog, where most things are murky and muddled and dull. Many emotions will be similar to those your depressed partner experiences. The difference is that you are not ill. You can do something about yours:

Accept that you have feelings

Give yourself permission to experience them. It's perfectly natural to be in an emotional turmoil at this time.

Express how you feel somehow

Tell someone, or write your feelings down. This makes things clearer for you, and helps to get things out in the open. This is important, because when negative emotions are not dealt with they can develop and fester into a malignant knot.

Avoid feeling guilty

Guilt is a totally useless emotion. It uses up loads of energy and is completely negative. If you find it tricky to avoid feeling guilty, try this: write down or say "I feel guilty." Now put "I choose" in front of it, so that you write or say "I choose to feel guilty" – because you *do* have a choice. There is no point in wishing you had or had not done or said something or other, and being full of regret. Whatever the reason for your guilt, you can now do something to make amends. So make a start and move forwards. If you feel guilty you are only ever looking backwards – and that's hopeless.

It can be helpful to be aware of the different emotions as you are experiencing them, so that you can start to deal with them. Here are some examples. You could probably add a few more.

loved	guilty	loathing	alone
rejected	unloving	patronised	fearful
sad	resentful	loving	perplexed
helpless	selfish	resented	cruel
demoralised	confident	unsupported	unloved
frustrated	impatient	empathetic	blamed
blaming	supporting	hated	unsympathetic
angry	confused	bewildered	despairing
hopeless	sympathetic	negative	loathed
ignored	exhausted	wounded	hatred
helpless	patronising	lonely	caring
ashamed	bitter	uncaring	accepting
unconfident	dejected	irritable	

Think about how you experience these emotions.

Whereabouts in your body do you feel them?

This is important, because it is to do with energy. Thoughts and feelings always bring about a physical reaction. Most of the emotions on this list are negative, therefore they will 'bring you down'. You may think about them in your head, but I'll bet the real feeling is in your solar plexus area and your throat. How does your voice sound? How is your appetite? You may feel tense in your shoulders and lower back too.

So how 'down' are you physically?

Notice your posture. Notice your face. When Jim was at his worst I caught a glimpse of myself in a mirror. I was really horrified! This was not a look in the mirror that I had planned or was ready for – it was just a random glimpse. My posture was a little downcast – but it was my face that shocked me. I looked pinched and drawn and I seemed to have aged considerably.

When I saw myself in the mirror, I realised that I could not go on as I was. I made a point of taking up yoga again, so that I got some 'me-time', and so that I could give my body a good stretch. I also had my hair done and bought some new make up. Those were very practical things that made me feel better.

Other things that you could do are:

- Any physical exercise. This will boost your energy and give you a lift.

- Pay attention to your physical appearance, and maybe try something new.

- Do something appropriate that you enjoy and that makes you feel good.

- Make a point of standing and sitting up straight. The upright nature of your posture has a real affect on you mentally and helps you to feel more upbeat. Your whole centre of energy seems to change.

For in depth, lasting work on body posture and energy, you may like to explore the Alexander Technique. This is a sophisticated yet simple method of learning to use your body in the most effective way possible. Under a qualified practitioner, you learn to adjust and correct postural habits so that you can move with greater ease and efficiency. This helps to release unwanted tension, and helps you to manage stress. Contact The Society of Teachers of the Alexander Technique.

www.stat.org.uk Tel: 0845 230 7828

All of the above will help to lift your spirits, energise you, and help you to keep a sense of perspective. They will reinforce the fact that you have a life apart from your depressed partner.

Chapter 13

So here he was, the man I loved – hating me, blaming me, accusing me – over and over again. A man in torment. Deranged. Was I really that bad, I wondered? All right, maybe I'd not been the perfect partner over the past twenty years. I was not completely without blame. I knew I could be tricky to live with, selfish and moody sometimes. But I was not the evil witch that he would have me believe. I'd loved and cared for him throughout our lives together. I'd had his children. He'd loved and cared for me. He'd looked after me through thick and thin. He'd always been there for me and we'd had loads of fun together. We had a life partnership, which had seemed to work so far.

So what on earth had happened? Why now, after all this, having loved and comforted him through his darkest hours, did he hate me so much? I felt as if I'd been slapped in the face, kicked in the teeth, and severely winded all at once.

Not everyone becomes angry

Everyone's experience of depression is different, and it may change as they sink into a deeper state of depression. Some people feel and exhibit anger, some do not. Many people do not have the energy to be angry. They may be in a state of lethargy and hopelessness.

Lena

Lena and Anna had been partners for several years. Lena told me:

"Anna had always had a tendency to get quite 'low' sometimes, but when her father died, she sank into depression. It was awful. She got so clingy. She drank quite a lot, and everything just seemed so black. She wouldn't go out in the evening – she just wanted to sit on the sofa with me and cry and cuddle. It was really tough at the time – she was so full of self-pity. She had no interest in what I was doing really. Sometimes I really felt like leaving. She had counselling, but I gather she just used to sit there and say nothing, 'cos she'd come home and say what a waste of time it was. But she kept going. Months later, she told her counsellor that she hadn't ever felt able to tell her parents about her sexuality. This seemed to be a key thing for her. Anyway, eventually she told them, and now she's fine. It was bloody awful living with her at the time though."

What you can do to help yourself:

Keep upbeat, and keep positive. The following will help:

- *Laugh* – as much as possible. The effects of this are even better when you share that laughter with someone else.

- *Sing* – even if you think you can't. What is considered tuneful in western culture, is not necessarily so in others. Therefore, everyone can sing. It's just a matter of what to sing. Many singing groups cover a range of material from all over the world, and there may be one that you could participate in near you. If you don't fancy this, sing to yourself – often.

Laughing and singing have a physical effect which will help to give you a boost.

Attempts at conversations were becoming a nightmare. *If* Jim wanted to talk to me, it was often late at night, when I was at my most tired. When I tried to talk to him he was usually busy or just about to go out somewhere. Sometimes I paved the way by saying something like:

"When you have a moment, I need to talk to you."

As soon as I said this his body would tense, and he was immediately suspicious.

"What about? Why do you need to talk to me?"

He looked as if I was about to shoot him. I only chose my words like this if I really did need to talk, for example if it was something important concerning our children. This way, at least I got his attention.

There were numerous times when our communication with each other seemed crazy. Jim's interpretation of whatever I said was often way off the mark. He made huge assumptions – most of which boiled down to the fact that he thought I was attacking him personally. For example, we went for a walk with one of our daughters. He went to the newsagents, and our daughter and I sat on a wall chatting, waiting for him. When he returned, she casually remarked:

"Dad's behind you mum." I turned around, surprised to see him standing where he was – right behind me.

"Oh – hello." I must have looked a bit taken aback, because he immediately seemed irritated.

"What's the matter?"

"Well, nothing – I was just surprised to see you standing there, that's all." I answered amiably (or so I thought). Immediately I realised I had said the wrong thing.

"Why shouldn't I stand here? Are you accusing me of standing here? I can stand where I want can't I? It's up to me…" Our daughter interrupted him:

"Dad," she said, "she was only speaking to you."

A sulky silence ensued and we went home.

It was as if we were involved in some bizarre verbal board game, which neither of us was allowed to win. Like this:

Instructions	Player	Communication
Both players in starting position: 9.30am *Caroline starts by asking a question.*	Caroline	"What are you doing today Jim?"
Caroline pick up 'Alert' card		*You've made a mistake – now face the consequences.* You should have noticed the signs: Jim freezes/body tenses/sighs. Eyes roll heaven-wards (optional)
	Jim	"I don't know. What do you want to know for anyway?"
	Caroline	"Well, I just wondered – I was interested, that's all."
	Jim	"I don't know, I haven't decided yet. When I do know, I'll tell you if it's so important to you. All right?"
Caroline pick up 'Choice' card		*Choose your response carefully*
	Caroline	(sighs) "I…"

Caroline pick up 'Alert' card		*This is not an acceptable response* (notice how annoyed it makes Jim)
	Jim	"Look, I asked you a question. Are you going to answer or not?"
	Caroline	"What question?"
	Jim	"You know what question. Or am I just talking to myself?"
	Caroline	"I don't know what you mean – look it doesn't matter. I only wondered if you'd any plans…"
	Jim	(Glares at Caroline, waiting for her answer.)
Caroline pick up 'Choice' card		*Choose your response carefully*
	Caroline	(Leaves room seething with frustration)
Caroline pick up 'Alert' card		*This is not an acceptable response* (notice how even more annoyed it makes Jim)
	Jim	"You always do this – say something and then go out of the room. You're not really interested in what I'm saying. Are you? Mmm?"

Caroline pick up 'Choice' card	*Choose your response carefully* (You may engage in further convoluted conversation, or you may walk away)

I walked away. I was fed up. Maybe I could have phrased the question in a more enabling way or something. Or perhaps it would have been better if I had just kept quiet. But I'd always talked to Jim. I'd asked him thousands of questions over the years – and got a reasonable response. We'd conversed and communicated about everything.

Now our communication was entirely different. Why had it become so complicated? Other couples managed to talk to each other. Other couples seemed to have conversations without having to plan, and weigh up the consequences of everything they said.

Actually, the reason for our breakdown in communication is fairly straightforward. Jim's view of the world had changed due to his 'black dog'. Mine had not.

> When someone is depressed they lock themselves into a much narrower view of the world than the one they had before. For example, they can niggle, and focus on small details, which to you may seem irrelevant. Alongside this rigid, blinkered way of thinking may develop a tendency to react quite abnormally to ordinary issues and events.
>
> If a person thinks that everything's gone wrong in their lives, they may think that this will always be the case. They may not be able to imagine that there can ever be anything different. A person who is depressed may jump to conclusions and make huge assumptions, only seeing the bad in everything.

> Also, negative thinking fuels *irrational* thinking. When someone thinks irrationally, they can blow things out of proportion, making things seem much worse than they really are. Of course, anyone may have a tendency to do this, but when a person is depressed they do it much more.

Jim and I no longer shared a similar view of the world. Imagine we had been placed on a see-saw together. I would have been in the middle – where I had always been – equidistant from each end, and balanced. He would have slid down towards the low end – his view of the world tainted by depression. This position had become his 'truth'. He experienced the world from that vantage point – but I didn't. I couldn't share his view of the world, and I didn't want to. I preferred mine. From where I was sitting, the world looked rich and full and bright. Therefore, not only were our conversations unwieldy, but we weren't actually communicating properly at all.

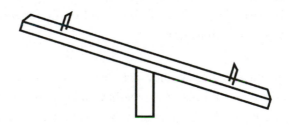

Chapter 14

I began to feel excluded. I felt I was no longer privy to any of Jim's activities, or the conversations he had with anyone else. He no longer discussed things with me. People presumed that I knew all sorts of things – things that I, as his partner, would expect to be aware of. Prior to his illness, I would have been. We would have had a conversation. He would have been open and up front. There wouldn't have been any secrets. But now I was living in a twilight zone. He either thought he had told me things, or he hadn't wanted me to know. There was no way that I could be sure. The point is that his life was becoming entirely separate from mine.

It's important to realise that someone who has been depressed for any length of time inhabits a different mental world from someone who has not. Their view of the world changes as they become fixed and focused on their own thoughts and feelings, and it may be that whatever you say makes no difference, or only serves to make them angry.

If the depressed person is your partner, I think it is as well to be aware of the following:

When their view of the world becomes so different from yours, a crack appears in the relationship. This could:

- close over as they recover, and your relationship may be strength-ened in the long run from it

- remain as a gap, that you are able to manage

- become a chasm

This is in no way intended to paint a bleak picture, but it was something that I never really took on board on first. I just thought, "Oh – Jim'll get better and everything will be OK."

However, on reflection, I remember a couple of people said: "You know he might not really get completely better," and "I think you'll just have to think about what you want to do…"

At the time, I didn't really *hear* what they were saying. Now, I think forewarned is forearmed.

You and your partner may want things to get back to normal, but having lived the depression experience, the 'normal' will have changed. Their experience will have coloured their thoughts, feelings and behaviour in some way. Their view of the world will have changed, and you will also have been affected. Depression is deep seated and far reaching. It leaves a legacy for both you and your partner in the form of memories, and of new (possibly negative) thought habits and patterns.

I wondered what Jim was saying to others about me. I started having quite irrational thoughts, such as:

"His family hate me. His friends hate me. I can't talk to them. I want to avoid them."

I was becoming paranoid – but surely this was ridiculous? Fortunately, the fact that his family was such a support made me realise that I had got it all wrong. When his friends phoned and spoke to me at length – even people I didn't really know well – I realised that whatever he might be saying was falling on deaf ears and, actually, they were concerned.

I did much soul-searching at that time. *Was* I manipulative? Was I impossibly controlling? I knew I was bossy sometimes, but manipulative? I hoped to God I was not that. I'd always loathed the way that some women tried to control and change their partners. Why would I want to manipulate Jim? What would be the point? I loved him because he was Jim, a man, my life partner – not a project that I'd created. My thoughts went round and round. I had no idea how to handle this. At least when Jim was miserable, I could hold him and offer some comfort. Now I seemed to be the *cause* of it. I didn't really know where to turn.

What you can do to help yourself:

Give yourself a mental break. Take some time to discover your own special place – somewhere that you love, that is good, and where you feel safe and at peace. Create your own sanctuary in your mind. This may be somewhere that you know, or somewhere that you invent. For example:

A beach with smooth white sand
A fabulous garden with flowers and trees
A wood with a stream
A cool and sunny ski slope
A wonderful room
A marble temple

- Find somewhere quiet. Close your eyes and, if possible, do the conscious relaxation on page 00 first.

- Imagine the place you've chosen, and be aware of as much detail as possible. Notice the climate, the colours, the sounds, scents and tastes. Make it just right for you. This is your own special sanctuary.

- Give yourself time to really experience this place. Really 'be' there.

- When you're satisfied that it is the best that it can be, just notice what stands out for you. Is there some aspect of it that you'll remember above everything else? You can use this to trigger the memory of this place again, and to fix you into it.

Once you've really got it, you'll get it again and be able to return there whenever you want.

This is a great way to take a mental rest from all the aggravation going on around you. With practice you can put yourself right back there in seconds – anywhere, and in the midst of everything.

What I really wanted was some guidance. I went to the doctor to ask him what to expect from this illness. He sat and listened to me, and nodded empathically. I left the surgery and realised that he'd not really offered any explanations, or advice. I don't think he could. He'd done his job really, referring Jim to a psychiatrist and counsellor.

At a later date, I went to the doctor again. This time I asked if *I* could have some counselling – to help me to get through all this. I really felt I needed someone to talk to – a professional who could understand. The doctor empathised, but couldn't really help. They had access to one counsellor, he said, and she was seeing Jim. It would be inappropriate for her to see me too.

"A conflict of interests you understand…maybe you could find someone privately?"

Well no, actually, I couldn't. Jim was signed off sick, and we had no spare cash.

"Bloody hell." I thought. "So what am I supposed to do?"

At least I could talk to Jim's sister and her husband for free. Well, the price of a phone call anyway. They assured me that I was not to blame. I was not the manipulative tyrant that he would have me believe. Deep inside of me I knew this, but I needed to hear it occasionally. I was in danger of being brainwashed by his vehement hatred and repeated accusations. Just to be told that actually I was OK, gave me such a boost.

I felt uneasy, and reluctant to talk to my family or friends about what was going on. I just had a sense that I was being disloyal – that I might be betraying Jim in some way. However, those I did tell were great, and very supportive in their own ways.

I talked to my daughters. After all, we were going through this together. As teenagers, I knew that their emotional development was vulnerable, so I always made sure we talked about dad with respect, and that I kept as upbeat as I could. Fortunately they understood that it was his illness that was the problem, not the man himself.

One day, in utter desperation I telephoned The Samaritans. I was so fed up I just had to talk to someone. The woman at the other end calmly responded as I offloaded my feelings for a few minutes. As I vented my spleen I began to feel better. Thank you Miss Anonymous. I really needed you that day.

www.samaritans.org Tel: (24 hour helpline) 08457 909090

Though it was so important to be able to share my thoughts and feelings with another person from time to time, what I really wanted more than anything else was some information. Not just about depression – there is a wealth of literature available about that. I wanted to know how to deal with Jim, how to cope. For example, when he was argumentative and accusatory:

- Should I be passive and just say "Yes dear," in the hope that he'd get bored and shut up?

- Or should I argue back and give him a run for his money?

❥ Should I be cruel and walk away leaving him talking to himself?

❥ Should I lock myself into a room or leave the house?

❥ Should I make a point of bursting into tears (God knows I wanted to often enough)?

What was the best way to respond, bearing in mind that our daughters were often in the house too? I didn't want them to be upset any more than they were anyway.

I really didn't know what to do for the best, and I'm sure I took all these options at one time or another. *The thing is, nobody else seemed to know either.*

There are no definitive right ways to deal with a depressed partner, as everyone is so different. So as you try out a few approaches, bear these things in mind:

● It is not the *person* but their *behaviour* that is the issue here. Keep your sense of perspective by recognizing that these are separate.

● Accept that your partner is depressed and so cannot help the way they behave.

● Be there for them and show compassion, because they need to know you care, even if they don't appear to acknowledge this.

● Refer to their strengths and achievements by reminding them what they are every so often. They need to hear this – even though you may not feel like telling them.

● Employ whatever tricks are necessary to enable you to cope.

What you can do to help yourself:

It's a waste of time to argue. You're unlikely to win against someone who is depressed and hostile. If you need to talk about something important, forget it while they're angry or agitated. Distance yourself mentally, and possibly physically, and choose another time.

Distancing yourself can be like playing a game.

You can simply go off and do something else. As you step out of the room or the area, take a deep breath in, and as you breathe out tell yourself mentally that you are stepping into a safe zone. You are physically leaving the aggravation behind.

If you are stuck in close proximity to the person, you can distance yourself mentally. While they are being foul, just think of something you like – a place or an object, or a tune maybe. See it, feel it, hear it. Whatever works for you. Keep it in mind somehow. It's amazing how you quickly you learn to appear to listen and respond when actually you aren't really paying attention.

In a way this suggestion goes against every wish to be helpful and kind to the person who is depressed. But negativity and hostility can grind you down into despair. This is about your survival, and sometimes you have to employ a few tricks.

Chapter 15

One day, I made a terrible blunder. Its impact has taken years to dispel. I had spent the weekend being verbally 'got at' by Jim. The girls had been a bit tearful. They hated this atmosphere. I had got to a point where I thought I just couldn't stand it anymore, and I remember grabbing my phone and driving to a relatively remote spot. In desperation, I phoned various members of the family to tell them my tales of woe. I was at my lowest point then, emotionally drained and exhausted:

"It's awful. I just don't know what to do…" I wailed. There were several offers to go and stay with people, but I needed to think. I didn't need to run away. Then I made a decision. I would speak to Jim's counsellor. Surely she would be able to tell me what sort of thing I had to expect, and how to cope with this nightmare? I waited until he was out, and then I picked up the telephone.

Amazingly, she did speak to me. I made it very clear that I had no intention of breaching any confidentiality, but I just wanted to know – what could I do? How could I help? Did she really know how he behaved at home? The counsellor was tactful and empathic – and that was it. No suggestions, no strategies. I'm not sure what I expected – I hadn't broken any rules by speaking to her, but I was still in turmoil.

Later, in the midst of another bizarre and irrational conversation with Jim, I unintentionally let it slip that I had been in touch with his counsellor. Understandably, he was absolutely livid. Any remaining sliver of trust he had had for me until that point vanished.

Things went from bad to worse really. We'd bicker hatefully over petty things. All I longed for was a relatively harmonious existence. Jim seemed to want to pick a fight over anything. I'm not sure that I handled things as well as I might have done. I think my reactions were not always helpful, and I probably added fuel to his already smouldering fire. Our domestic life had shrunk into endless misunderstandings, trivial arguments and grievances.

For example, I usually did the washing – sorting the clothes and loading the machine. I always had done, and it was second nature. Now, for some reason, Jim decided that he would do this, while I was at work. The clothes were all crammed into the machine together, and emerged looking as if they'd come out of a rubbish bag.

"Bloody hell," I thought, as I looked at my delicate blouse which hung limply over the rail. When I'd put it in the washing basket it was white. Now it was faintly blue-grey. The fabric had screamed out:

'Hand wash only. Wash separately.'

I was furious. I'd had a busy day and I didn't need this. I felt my face burn with indignation. I wanted to yell and accuse Jim: "Why didn't you leave it? What were you thinking of?" but I thought better of it, and locked myself in the lavatory. Later on that evening I casually-on-purpose mentioned:

"Oh – you did the washing."

"Yes?" he said defensively. I chose my words carefully, thanking him first. And then, keeping upbeat and matter-of-fact I explained that it worked better if clothes were separated into colours, and that different fabrics required a different wash. Whoops! Big mistake. I'd said "it worked *better.*" How stupid was that? And how patronising? Of course Jim felt attacked, and he fired back:

"You're always so bloody self-righteous." That was the end of any further interaction between us that evening.

Jim continued to do the washing whenever he felt like it, and glared at me defiantly whenever I walked past the drying clothes. What point was he trying to make, I wondered? Perhaps he really wanted to help. Maybe he wanted to prove that he was in control or something. Nevertheless, I wasn't going to risk my expensive shirts, and the girls' new tops. So I took to hiding them as damage limitation, and washed them myself later.

Our relationship was deteriorating fast. Almost everything I said either irritated Jim or made him really angry. It was like treading on eggshells – I never knew how he would react. Any remark I made could mean that I'd misjudged a situation, and said the wrong thing at the wrong time. He'd react by sighing and rolling his eyes. Then he would either pre-empt what I was going to say and finish my sentence, or imitate me after I'd spoken – like a child imitating a teacher. I was accused of being impatient and intolerant. I was told I had 'the gift of the gab'. Why? How? What did he mean? I was completely at a loss to understand.

What you can do to help yourself:

When you're in the thick of the situation – stand back. Remove yourself emotionally to avoid getting drawn into an argument. One of the ways you can do this is by observing your partner as if you were studying a dance.

Imagine you are about to give an account of what you see. So notice:

What are they doing?

How are they doing it? How much energy are they using? What kind of speed? Is there a rhythm?

Where are they? Where are they in terms of space to you? How big are the spaces in between you both?

Who or What are they relating to? Is it you? Is it them?

This is quite an interesting thing to do. You can learn a thing or two about where your partner is placing their time, energy and attention.

I constantly questioned myself. Was it the way I was saying things, or the *content* that annoyed him so much? Was I missing the point completely here? How, after all these years, had I changed? Or had I annoyed him so much for years, and not realised it?

I was so sick of this. If it was just occasional petty squabbling I might have felt differently. But this was much more serious.

I had to remind myself that Jim was ill, and that the way that he was acting was as a result of that. I also noticed that the behaviour he demonstrated was often exactly that of which he accused *me*. Aggie Armstrong's 'cruel bastard – that black dog' was certainly showing what it was capable of.

I loved Jim, but I hated what he was doing. It is essential to separate the person from their behaviour. Behaviour can change. The core qualities that are part of a person are still usually there, underneath a 'mish-mash' of thoughts and feelings. What you see and have to deal with is the behaviour that comes about as a result. It can be really tricky to separate the person from their behaviour – but this is what you have to do.

Things had definitely changed for both of us. At first I really cared. I wanted to help so much. But once the anger and the accusations started – and continued – I couldn't wait to get away. Going to work became my refuge. I made extended trips to the supermarket on my way home, to prolong the normality in the day. Our daughters seemed to manage, but I hated that fact that they had to live with this. The atmosphere in our home was awful. Though Jim largely kept himself to one room, his persona filled the house.

> When a person who is depressed experiences strong feelings of low self-esteem and inadequacy, they may appear callous or unemotional. This is a cover for their turmoil and pain. It is horrible to be at the receiving end of this, and it may go on for some time.

Once the anger had taken hold, most of the respect Jim and I had for each other left. I didn't want to be in the same room as him, let alone bed. There was now a mutual lack of trust. I had no idea how he might react next and, actually, I didn't really care any more.

"No one should have to live with someone who hates them." I thought.

I never really felt that leaving was an option. What, when all was said and done, would have been the point? And who would have benefited? Jim was ill and troubled – not evil. Why disrupt our lives again? We all loved Jim really. We just wanted him back.

In some ways living with someone you love who becomes depressed, can be like bereavement. You go through emotional turmoil. You think "if only…" and "I wish…" and you crave the life you had with them. Of course that person is still alive – but your lives together may never be quite the same.

I felt that I grieved. Sometimes I did wonder how life would have been if Jim had died. I even wondered if I was being prepared in some way. I think that by going through this process I gained the strength to stand back and to separate myself, so that we could remain as a family and get on with our lives.

Fiona

Fiona's partner suffered with arthritis. Usually very loving and attentive, he suddenly changed. She said:

"He's prone to low moods anyway and his arthritis is always worse when he is in mental distress. A few weeks ago he became extremely withdrawn quite suddenly – hardly spoke, wouldn't look at me, didn't touch me or kiss me goodbye, didn't call (he usually rings a couple of times a day from work, just to say hello), wouldn't eat and avoided sex. After a miserable weekend I confronted him. He broke down, and said he knew he was depressed. He felt there was no point to anything, and that he was dragging himself through every day. The next day he just went to pieces. I was really supportive, but I needed to get some shopping, and he begged me not to leave him, as he said he didn't feel safe. He came with me in the end. But he refused to seek help.

When I tried to talk to him about it he told me to stop fussing, and that he could sort it out. He didn't seem able to appreciate how this was affecting me. I felt so drained, hurt, rejected, fed up and angry. I was sure his arthritis was a major cause of his depression, but he really thought he could get better on his own, and that I should be patient until he had sorted himself out, no matter how long it took. But I knew that he was internalising and brooding, which would only make things worse."

In time Fiona's partner seemed better. However, the experience left her feeling traumatised and insecure. She said:

"I no longer feel completely safe. Before he was depressed our relationship was exceptionally close and happy. I felt secure and trusted him

completely. He was always there to talk to about anything – he was my best friend. I am grateful and feel lucky that this episode was short and on the surface things have pretty much returned to normal. However, I feel much more insecure than I used to. I questioned what else was possible if he could change so dramatically. I feel that I can take nothing for granted."

Chapter 16

In the fullness of time, Jim gradually got better. He stopped going away so much, and started doing things around the house. He busied himself with various projects, and he seemed calmer. I reckon it was about nine months to a year before I was aware of a significant difference in his persona. During this time I had come to realise that his depression must have been building up for years, and that it would probably take years to go. If it ever did. I'd almost got used to the horribleness, and the unpredictability.

He was still quite unpleasant and accusatory towards me. I felt that the rift that developed between us had now become a chasm. Though we lived together, we now led totally separate lives. He told me little about his plans and thoughts, but if something bothered him he made sure I knew.

It occurred to me that my work must have been something of a mystery to him. We had hardly discussed what I was doing and what it entailed. If he asked me something, I tended to keep my answers to the minimum in order to avoid saying the wrong thing. Sometimes, I really wanted to tell him things – but I always weighed up the pros and cons before I spoke. I just couldn't be bothered with the hassle of the conversation. We were still playing bizarre verbal board games when we spoke to each other. Consequently, we conversed, but rarely communicated properly.

Whenever I did talk to Jim, I noticed that he sat with his arms folded, looking downward. This drove me to distraction. In body language terms, I understood that his folded arms might mean, "I'm protecting myself from whatever you're going to throw at me." On the other hand, he may just have been more comfortable like that. But it was the fact that he didn't look at me that made me want to scream.

At the time I took the downcast eyes as meaning that he was not really listening and not interested. This led to my feeling rejected and undervalued. I dealt with this by avoiding conversations, and bottling things up.

Later, I learnt that some people listen more effectively when they look down. It's all to do with how they personally process information. But if your way of processing information is different, they can drive you mad. I spent most conversations glaring at Jim, feeling more and more frustrated and wanting to shout: "Well, look at me then!"

> We all process information differently and this can lead to misunderstandings. We know that eye contact is important, because it gives the person talking a signal – proof that they are being listened to. But it's worth bearing in mind that some people have to work really hard at creating that eye contact, as it does not come naturally when they are *really listening.*

I had always been infuriated by Jim's ability to sulk. If in the past we'd had an argument, he would dwell on it for hours – days sometimes, whilst I would be ready to forgive and forget quite quickly. It was many years before I realised that my instantly sunny 'kiss and make up' approach may have been adding to his angst.

It was something of a revelation to me to discover that some people need to dwell on things. It's part of the way they process information in order to deal with it. They need time to 'lick their wounds.' I was a person who, once the argument had taken place, was ready to make amends whatever the outcome. When I was furious, I would blow up – and then I'd say sorry and expect everything to be fine again, in much the same way as a child might do. So of course, I was exasperated when Jim would not reciprocate. Now I realise that he just couldn't. It simply was not in his nature, and on the occasions when he tried to appease me by agreeing to be friends again, it didn't really work. He was still smouldering and inwardly digesting our argument through his smiles.

I am aware of my own shortcomings, and I am not particularly proud of them. I can be foul tempered, foul mouthed, judgemental and selfish. I can make huge assumptions, and sometimes I talk over the top of others. I can be quite childish – though I am a mature woman. I have loads of good qualities as well, which is probably why Jim chose to spend his life with me.

I chose Jim because he is a wonderful person. Through his depression, his practical skills never left him, and the personal characteristics that attracted me so much in the first place, just became blurred. Apart from a few months when he was at his most savagely depressed, he continued to do all the things he has always done in the family as gardener, children's chauffeur, car maintainer, painter, plumber, electrician, handyman, joiner, extension-builder, cook, financial organiser and so on.

The practical skills were always in place. Jim is exceptionally good at these things – so much so that other women have sometimes said, "Oh you are lucky." to which my response has usually been:

"Luck's got nothing to do with it. I knew what I was getting – after all, I chose him."

I *did* choose Jim. I knew exactly what I was getting. We'd lived together for eight years before we married and so there were few surprises for either of us – until this depression. He was highly intelligent with a sense of adventure and fun, and an acerbic sense of humour. I particularly valued his kind, caring, gentle and attentive nature.

It was these latter qualities in particular that became obscured by depression – and I missed them so much. To be honest, over the ensuing months and years I got so used to our ambiguous communication patterns that I didn't expect anything different. I knew that he cared really, and that he found expressing emotions more challenging since he had been depressed.

What you can do to help yourself:

Do something creative, or something that stretches you mentally.

- One person I spoke to did a crossword each evening. He said he found it therapeutic. Another kept a jigsaw on the go and returned to it several times a day.

- Some people find keeping a journal useful. It's a good way to notice your own patterns of stress. There's something about seeing things written down that really helps.

- Any creative writing can be good – poetry for example.

- Some people paint wonderful pictures, others do embroidery.

- A friend of mine designs clothes.

These are examples – any creative pursuit has a therapeutic element. Above all, it will give you some time just for yourself.

Chapter 17

Time went on and, although Jim was to all intents and purposes better, we still had crazy misunderstandings and bizarre conversations. We went round and round and backward, but rarely forward. The whole communication thing was still pretty unproductive, and quite often I seemed to make him hopping mad.

For example, I rarely got a straight answer when I asked for help or advice. Jim seemed utterly baffled as to why I didn't know the answer already. He'd sigh impatiently, roll his eyes and say something like:

"*Surely* you know how to…"

Then he'd make a big deal about stopping whatever he was doing, and bluster about – tossing remarks at me intermittently: "*Surely* you remember…I just *assumed* you knew…"

And then a few minutes later: "I don't understand how you can't know…"

At first, I used to think:

"No Jim, I don't bloody well know. In fact I wish I'd never asked." I never *said* this though. I'd learnt not to react by retaliating. It simply wasn't worth it. If I wanted something, it was easier just to acquiesce.

The bizarre verbal board games continued. They became normal in our lives. I knew roughly what to expect, and it didn't really bother me any more. The difference was that I approached Jim less.

Many comments that I meant to be helpful were taken by Jim as if they were a personal attack. He sometimes retaliated by referring to small misdemeanours of mine from twenty to thirty years ago. I found it hard to believe that he had remembered any of these. But worse – he bore a grudge for something I'd said then, or a letter I'd written. I'd think to myself:

"For God's sake. We've brought up a family since then. People change and life moves on. Why do you do this?"

What you can do to help yourself:

You may keep replaying things that your partner said and did after the event. Help yourself to take one step back and remove yourself emotionally from the situation like this:

- Imagine you are watching TV, or that you are in a projection room in a cinema. Either way there is a pane of glass between you and the picture you are about to see. You have a control switch in your hand.

- Now let the picture start. Play whichever memory bothers you – the one where your partner was particularly sad, or unkind. See your partner and yourself, and watch what was going on in that scene.

- Look at the picture. Is it colour or black and white?

- Turn up the sound with your control switch. Or turn it down if you want.

- Is the picture fuzzy or clear? Adjust it if you want.

- You can alter the speed if you want – slow motion or very fast.

- Replay it as many times as you like.

- Try playing it backwards.

- Turn it off when you've had enough. You have the control switch. You can watch it, or not. It's your choice.

- Now put the control switch down and walk away. Go and do something that you like.

There now. You've looked at the whole thing again. You looked at it through glass. You weren't involved. Just notice how you feel now.

Several months later, Jim, the girls and I had a huge treat. We went to New York for the weekend. We had a great time, and Jim seemed to be almost like his old self. However when we came back, the tiny freezer on top of the fridge had almost defrosted. Jim was furious. In a frenzied state he started to chip at the remaining ice.

"Someone left the door open. Why did you not all check? This could've been avoided…" On and on he went. We hadn't even taken off our coats. Maybe this was as well, as although the house was warm, the atmosphere was as cold as the freezer.

What you can do to help yourself:

Small things can become hugely important to someone who is depressed, and this can have a real impact on you. Like Jim and the freezer – no one had intentionally left the door open, despite what he thought. It was nobody's 'fault'.

If something *is* your fault you can do something about it. If something is the fault of a person's illness and depression (such as the way they behave), there may be little that you can do for them at that moment. But you can manage the way you deal with your own feelings about it.

I used to speak silently to Jim when he behaved like this. It all took place in my head:

"The way you are behaving is irrational. I know that this is a result of your depression. You are getting on my nerves, but I'm going to ignore that. I will answer if you want me to, and I will say whatever you want to hear in order to shut you up. But I will not let you spoil things for me (or the children)."

Two years later, we had a real family holiday on a Greek Island. We had a terrific apartment with a pool. It was wonderful. Jim loved the heat and appeared to be very relaxed. He insisted on taking himself to the beach at the hottest point in the day, and only seemed mildly offended that none of us wanted to go with him. (He has olive, sun-friendly skin. I and the girls are so pale that we are almost transparent. We prefer the shade.) So all was going well – until one evening, somewhere around the start of the second week, when I made the foolish mistake of asking Jim what he'd like to eat.

"I don't know – I can't think about it now." he shouted angrily.

Somewhat taken aback, I prepared some food and the girls and I sat down to have our meal. Jim came in.

"Would you like some of this?" I asked. Whoops! Colossal mistake.

"What's this obsession with food?" he yelled. "All I hear you talk about is food. All the time."

I saw the girls' faces fall. This was all too familiar.

"I only asked you if you wanted some of this." I answered. I was really shocked. His reaction was like a bolt out of the blue.

Jim hardly spoke to me for two days after that. He hardly spoke to the girls either. They still mention this incident occasionally – though not to him. It seemed that it never occurred to Jim that we might have been hurt or upset. It infuriated and exasperated the girls. There was never any apology, and never an explanation. It showed yet again how fragile relationships can be, and how tenuous the link is between happiness and misery.

What you can do to help yourself:

Last thing at night, let your thoughts go. This is easier said than done I know, but it's actually a skill that you can learn and practice.

- Imagine a large wooden chest with a hinged open lid. (This is the equivalent of your subconscious mind.)

- Make a decision to put all the thoughts that are bothering you into that box.

- Put your thoughts in, one by one. You might like to give each thought a different colour or shape. As you do so, feel that you have released those thoughts. Be firm and authoritative and determined.

- Put the lid down firmly. You've given the thoughts to your subconscious to deal with, so you can go to sleep.

In the morning you may see things more clearly.

One day, we had a family dinner. There was a pleasant atmosphere, until I said something or other, and then – *snap*. Jim stomped off, leaving us all at the table, stunned and bewildered. What on earth had happened there? What had I said? I had no idea what had offended him. Needless to say, the dinner just petered out. We all left the table one by one as we finished. I had indigestion and Jim sulked for the rest of the evening.

What you can do to help yourself:

If you feel negative and angry, have a purge:

- Write your partner a letter explaining exactly how you feel.

- Now burn it.

Similarly:

- Write down each thought on a separate piece of paper.

- Now burn each one.

This can work well. It's a kind of ritualistic parting – separating you from your unwanted thoughts.

Various alternative and complementary approaches can be fantastically effective in the treatment of depression. Interestingly, many of these are older than modern western medicine. Some have to be paid for privately, and some insurance schemes cover a percentage of selected therapies. Many of the therapies are really helpful for partners of depressed people too. They can:

- help to boost the immune system – which you need to keep you going and help you to cope

- unblock energy systems in the body – without which you can feel so washed out and not be sure why

- help you to relax – and thereby have some time for yourself

The following approaches are amongst my favourites. They have all had particular success when dealing with someone who is depressed.

Hypnotherapy

Hypnotherapy involves helping the person to relax their body, and their conscious mind, so much that it becomes passive and quiet. The therapist can then access the subconscious easily, and talk to it in order to bring about change. This is usually done in one of two ways:

Suggestion hypnosis is when the therapist uses language skilfully in order to introduce beneficial suggestions to the subconscious. The subconscious will only accept these if it wants to.

Regression hypnosis is when the therapist causes the person to regress to an earlier memory or series of memories. Often a specific event or trauma is responsible for the issue that the person now faces, and it is quite likely to have first occurred when they were very young.

For example, a person may have witnessed or been subjected to something that affected them deeply when they were a child. They may have forgotten all about this, yet it has led to difficulties for them in later life – such as being depressed. Once this memory is rediscovered whilst under hypnosis, the subconscious, guided by the therapist, can fix it.

www.general-hypnotherapy-register.com Tel: 01590 683770

Also see the General Hypnotherapy Standards Council:
www.ghsc.co.uk

Neuro-Linguistic Programming (NLP)

NLP is about how you think, communicate and behave. It is to do with your use of language, and the way that you process information through your senses. It is to do with planning and achieving your goals, and moving forward in your life. Specific tools and methods have been devised that enable you to do this, and these can be applied to almost all areas of life. There is a huge amount of information available on NLP on the internet. If you wish to find a practitioner, try:

Association for Neuro-Linguistic Programming
www.anlp.org Tel: 0870 444 0790

Nutrition

What a person eats and drinks affects their health and well-being, often far more than they realise. Mental and physical illness and disorder can be prevented, relieved and often cured with the right diet. Increasing media coverage has been given to this subject over recent years, which has helped to build a general awareness.

Nutritional therapists are specially trained to work out exactly what an individual needs, and where they may have deficiencies, or even allergies. (An allergy or intolerance to wheat can be quite common in people who are depressed.) Depression, anxiety and stress eats up and diminishes a range of vital nutrients in the body, and these need to be identified and replaced. So a consultation with a nutritional therapist can sort this out properly. This is much more effective than guessing what your partner needs, and buying them a bottle of multivitamins. A good starting point is The British Association of Nutritional Therapists (BANT), **www.bant.org.uk** Tel: 08706 061284

Or The Institute for Optimum Nutrition: **www.ion.ac.uk**

Homeopathy

Homeopathy has been used in the UK for over two hundred years, though its origins go back to ancient Greece. Remedies are made from plant, mineral, metal and insect sources. These are prescribed in various dilutions and potencies, stimulating the body to heal itself. Homeopathy works on the principle that 'like cures like'. In other words, a condition can be treated by a substance that would produce similar symptoms in a healthy person. Therefore in order to prescribe an appropriate remedy, the homeopath treats each person as an individual case, looking at every aspect of that person's life – the physical, mental, emotional and spiritual. A remedy that is prescribed for one person may be different from that prescribed for another who has similar symptoms.

As a young woman I developed General Anxiety Disorder. It affected my life for two years until I discovered homeopathy. Within one month of consulting a homeopath and taking the prescribed remedy I was cured. Not just better, but cured.

www.homeopathy-soh.org Tel: 0845 450 6611

Acupuncture

This system of healing has been used in Eastern countries for thousands of years. It is a holistic form of healing, based on the philosophy that qi (vital energy) flows smoothly through channels (meridians) under the skin. Qi consists of the opposite qualities of yin and yang. When these are not in balance, a person may become ill. Many physical and emotional factors can interrupt the balance of qi. Fine needles are inserted into the channels of energy to stimulate the body to heal itself and rebalance its energy flow.

British Acupuncture Council, 63 Jeddo Road, London, W12 9HQ, UK. **www.acupuncture.org.uk** Tel: 020 8735 0400

If you or your partner are interested in looking at alternative approaches, please be aware of the following:

- Your depressed partner needs to consult a doctor in the first instance, to eliminate any physical reasons for the symptoms they are experiencing.

- When selecting a practitioner, make sure that they are properly qualified by checking their credentials against a centrally recognised register.

Chapter 18

Now, after several years, things have improved. Jim and I get along most of the time. Most people would never know there'd been anything wrong. But we do.

I notice that:

When things go wrong for him, Jim can quickly become very negative and down. However, he is usually aware of this now, and is able to do something about it before it gets out of hand. For example, he might do some physical activity, or talk to a friend.

Jim can switch from being pleasant to being argumentative and obsessive within minutes. A couple of well-chosen sentences from him can make us all feel fed up and low. Life with Jim can still sometimes be like treading on eggshells.

When Jim is stressed he can quickly slip into foul mode again. If I say or do the wrong thing, he tells me so repeatedly. Any verbal interaction between us is then a disaster. He gets so exasperated with me that what he says doesn't make sense.

The amount of resentment that built up within me as a result of Jim's depression was astonishing. For a while it permeated most areas of my life. I think much of this could have been avoided if I'd understood more about the effects of depression generally.

I am now able to 'switch off' quite easily. This is not because I don't care – because I do. It's just that I have a life of my own. I accept that in many respects Jim's view of the world is quite different from mine. And that's fine.

The wonderful personal qualities that attracted me to Jim in the first place are all still there. It's just that for a time, many of them were eclipsed by depression. As time has gone on, I've noticed that each one shines through a little more.

Jim's depression affected all of us. It was horrible at the time. Now, I want to thank Jim for going through it. By experiencing depression he gave me the opportunity to grow and become stronger. He gave me an insight into others which I did not have before. He made me realise that the really important part of a person never changes – it just gets obscured sometimes. He made me remember – because at times I forgot – that he is still the man I love.

The Black Dog's Dinner

A quick guide to help you avoid feeling chewed up and spat out

- Hang on to the fact that there are thousands, probably millions of people at this very moment who feel just like you do. They are experiencing similar emotions, thinking similar thoughts, and desperately wanting answers too.

- Always remember that it is the behaviour not the person that is the issue.

- Work at keeping your own protective bubble around you, so that your partner's negativity and/or anger cannot get through and wear you down.

- Learn to distance yourself whilst remaining compassionate.

- Keep upbeat and positive.

- Acknowledge that change is taking place for both of you. Accept that fact.

- Expect anything and everything.

Useful Contacts

We've put together a list of useful organisations to contact if you are trying to cope with a depressed partner. As contact details often change we've put the list on our website where we can update it regularly, rather than printed it here. You can find the list at **www.whiteladderpress.com**; click on 'useful contacts' next to the information about this book.

If you don't have access to the Internet you can contact White Ladder Press by any of the means listed on the next page and we'll print off a hard copy and post it to you free of charge.

Contact us

You're welcome to contact White Ladder Press if you have any questions or comments for either us or the authors. Please use whichever of the following routes suits you.

Phone: 01803 813343

Email: enquiries@whiteladderpress.com

Fax: 01803 813928

Address: White Ladder Press, Great Ambrook, Near Ipplepen, Devon TQ12 5UL

Website: www.whiteladderpress.com

What can our website do for you?

If you want more information about any of our books, you'll find it at **www.whiteladderpress.com**. In particular you'll find extracts from each of our books, and reviews of those that are already published. We also run special offers on future titles if you order online before publication. And you can request a copy of our free catalogue.

Many of our books have links pages, useful addresses and so on relevant to the subject of the book. You'll also find out a bit more about us and, if you're a writer yourself, you'll find our submission guidelines for authors. So please check us out and let us know if you have any comments, questions or suggestions.

What shall we do with Mother?

What to do when your elderly parent is dependent on you

All your life your parents have been capable adults, looking after themselves and, indeed, looking after you when you needed it.

And then you start to notice – often after your other parent's death – that your mum or dad is beginning to flounder. Maybe their health is starting to go or, frighteningly, their mind.

What Shall We Do With Mother? tells the stories of six people in just your situation, each struggling to care for a mother or father who increasingly needs their help. It passes on their experience, mistakes and advice for coping with:

- the dilemma of whether to put them in a home
- family pressures and conflicting demands on your time
- balancing what's best for them with what's best for you
- parents who develop difficult personalities or dementia
- the inevitable guilt that besets everyone in your position

Above all, their stories reassure you that you're not alone and there is a way through, to give your mum or dad the support they need without having to sacrifice your own sanity.

£9.99

Upping Sticks

How to move house and stay sane

They say moving house is one of the most stressful things you'll ever do. And they're not kidding.

Buying *or* selling is bad enough, but you're probably doing both. And if you're moving with children or animals the stakes get even higher. Mortgage problems, buyers who pull out, chains, dealing with solicitors, leaving a house you love, settling kids into a new school... yep, it's no surprise it's so stressful.

Which is why applied psychologists Sandi Mann and Paul Seager have come to your aid. They are here to help you move with the minimum of stress. They've drawn on information from their own survey of house movers and what makes their blood boil, and they bring you loads of tips, character profiles, case studies and checklists to help you relax and stay chilled as you:

- sell your home
- find and buy the new house
- cope with moving day
- get children – and even pets – through the move
- settle in and meet the neighbours

Use this guide and you'll be able to kick off your shoes, pour yourself a glass of wine and relax. You'll be one of those rare people who knows how to move house and stay sane.

£7.99